EDEXCEL

AS LEVEL
MUSIC

Revision
Guide

First published 2017 in Great Britain by
Rhinegold Education
14-15 Berners Street
London W1T 3LJ, UK
www.rhinegoldeducation.co.uk

© 2017 Rhinegold Education
a division of Music Sales Limited

You should always check the current
requirements of your examination,
since these may change.

Editor: Thomas Lydon
Cover and book design: Fresh Lemon Australia

Edexcel AS Level Music Revision Guide
Order No. RHG343
ISBN: 978-1-78558-171-7

Exclusive Distributors:
Music Sales Ltd
Distribution Centre, Newmarket Road
Bury St Edmunds, Suffolk IP33 3YB, UK

Printed in the EU

EDEXCEL

AS LEVEL MUSIC

Revision Guide

ALISTAIR WIGHTMAN

RHINEGOLD
EDUCATION

Contents

Introduction 5

Set works 17

Area of Study 1: Vocal music

Cantata 'Ein feste Burg ist unser Gott' BWV 80 (Bach),
1st, 2nd and 8th movements 17

Die Zauberflöte, excerpts from Act 1 (Mozart) 21

Area of Study 2: Instrumental music

Concerto in D minor Op. 3 No. 11 RV 565 (Vivaldi) 26

Piano Trio in G minor Op. 17, 1st movement (Clara Schumann) 30

Area of Study 3: Music for film

Cues from *The Duchess* (2008) (Rachel Portman) 34

Cues from *Batman Returns* (1992) (Danny Elfman) 38

Area of Study 4: Popular music and jazz

Tracks from *Back in the Day* (Courtney Pine) 43

Tracks from *Hounds of Love* (Kate Bush) 47

Area of Study 5: Fusions

Estampes, Nos. 1 and 2 (Debussy) 54

Tracks from *Caña Quema* (La Familia Valera Miranda) 60

Area of Study 6: New directions

Three Dances for Two Prepared Pianos, No. 1 (John Cage) 64

Petals [for Cello Solo and Optional Electronics] (Kaija Saariaho) 67

Sample materials for Question 6 72

Glossary 106

The author

Alistair Wightman

has worked in primary, secondary and further education, and is now a freelance teacher and writer. For many years he was a principal examiner in history and analysis in A Level music.

His publications include *Writing about Music* (Rhinegold, 2008) and several books and articles on Polish music, including *Karlowicz, Young Poland and the Musical Fin-de-siecle* (Ashgate, 1996), *Karol Szymanowski: his Life and Music* (Ashgate, 1999), *Szymanowski on Music: Selected Writings of Karol Szymanowski* (Toccata Press, 1999), and *Szymanowski's King Roger, the opera and its origins* (Toccata Press, 2015).

Edexcel AS Music (Code 8MU0) has three components:

1. **Performing**	Recorded recital	**60 marks:** 30% of the total AS mark
2. **Composing**	Two compositions	**60 marks:** 30% of the total AS mark
3. **Appraising**	Written examination	**80 marks:** 40% of the total AS mark

This guide will help you revise for **Component 3,** an externally assessed examination that lasts an hour and a half. The main focus will be on **Section B** (Extended Response), which requires you to answer a question about various musical features of the set works.

Pages 11–16 contain an overview of the terminology that will be used in the Section B (essay 2) questions, along with a list of the features you would be expected to mention in your answers.

On pages 17–71 are revision notes for each of the set works, giving some brief historical context, followed by pointers to the most important technical features of the music:

- Rhythm and metre
- Melody
- Harmony
- Tonality
- Texture
- Performance resources
- Music notation
- Structure.

The final sections of the book comprise sample essay questions and responses, followed by a glossary.

For practice materials for Sections A and B (essay 1), i.e. the listening questions, consult Rhinegold Education's *Edexcel AS/A level Music Listening Tests 2016*.

The marks for **Component 3** total 80, with the following breakdown:

Section A	Listening	**45 marks**
Section B	Essay 1 (Relating an unfamiliar extract to set works)	**15 marks**
Section B	Essay 2	**20 marks**

At the start of the summer term, it is quite likely that you will still be finishing Components 1 and 2. It is in your interest to complete these assignments as soon as you can, in order to maximise the time available for preparing for the Unit 3 examination.

Set works

With the exception of the dictation test, the whole of the Component 3 written examination revolves around the **prescribed works** in the *Edexcel AS/A level Anthology of Music*. You are required to study **all** the works within the six Areas of Study listed below.

Section A consists of three listening tests with skeleton scores and recordings, which cover three of the set works (in addition to the dictation text).

For **Section B (essay 1)**, you have to listen to an extract of unfamiliar music, which you then relate to appropriate set works.

For **Section B (essay 2)**, you answer one of three questions on set works. No recordings are available for this question, but you will have a resource booklet that contains a printed extract, if not the whole of the work. Consequently, you will be expected to depend on your knowledge of the work as a whole, as you may not have the complete score to hand.

The set works for AS are divided into six genres:

Vocal music
■ Cantata 'Ein feste Burg ist unser Gott' BWV 80, 1st, 2nd and 8th movements (Bach)
■ *Die Zauberflöte*, excerpts from Act I: No. 4 'Queen of the Night' and No. 5 'Quintet' (Mozart)

Instrumental music

- Concerto in D minor Op. 3 No. 11 RV 565 (Vivaldi)

- Piano Trio in G minor Op. 17, 1st movement (Clara Schumann)

Music for film

- Cues from *The Duchess* (2008): 'The Duchess' (Opening and End titles), 'Mistake of your life', 'Six years later' and 'Never see your children again' (Rachel Portman)

- Cues from *Batman Returns* (1992): Main theme ('Birth of a Penguin Part II'), 'Birth of a Penguin Part I', 'Batman vs the Circus' and 'The Rise and Fall from Grace' (Danny Elfman)

Popular music and jazz

- Tracks from *Back in the Day*: 'Lady Day and (John Coltrane)', 'Inner State (of Mind)' and 'Love and affection' (Courtney Pine)

- Tracks from *Hounds of Love*: 'Cloudbusting', 'And Dream of Sheep' and 'Under Ice' (Kate Bush)

Fusions

- *Estampes*, Nos. 1 and 2 ('Pagodes' and 'La Soirée dans Grenade') (Debussy)

- Tracks from *Caña Quema*': Allá va candela' and 'Se quema la chumbambá' (La Familia Valera Miranda)

New directions

- Three Dances for Two Prepared Pianos, No. 1 (John Cage)

- *Petals* (Kaija Saariaho)

Section A: Listening

In the exam you can listen to a short extract from the selected set works as many times as you wish. (Take care to manage the time available to your best advantage.) You will be provided with a single-line skeleton score of the extract, showing locations of the features you have to describe.

You will have to demonstrate your analytical knowledge and aural skills by identifying aspects such as:

- Instruments and/or voices
- Textures
- Rhythmic devices and patterns
- Melodic aspects
- Features of word-setting
- Keys, cadences and chords
- Harmonic devices
- Structure of the extract
- Location of the extract within the work.

By the time you take the exam, you should be totally familiar with the music, and be able to rely on analytical information you have already absorbed. Remember, though, that the extract's bar numbering may not correspond with the numbering in the Anthology.

Top tips

You should practise for the Section A exam as often as you can. Make sure you get in the habit of:

- Seeing how many marks are available for each question (and therefore how much information is required)
- Working out plausible possibilities (such as related keys) to support your impressions
- Using correct terms (keep referring to the terminology chapter on pages 11–16 of this book) to avoid long-winded explanations
- Using strategies in dictation tests to enable you to maximise your mark, such as:
  - First noting the number of sounds you hear by jotting down a dot for each note,
  - Working out where the bar lines fall, and then establishing individual note lengths
  - Charting pitches, being mindful of surrounding melody notes in the given parts

- In the 'error-spotting' test, follow the given part closely to detect pitch differences and changes in rhythmic patterns (perhaps insertion or removal of dotted rhythms or reversals of note-lengths).

Useful resources are the Sample Assessment Materials provided by Edexcel (ISBN 978-1-4469-3192-9) and Rhinegold Education's *Edexcel AS/A Level Music Listening Tests* 2016 (RHG 342).

Section B: Extended responses

In this section you answer **two** questions. The first of these is a listening test, which requires you to respond to a piece of unfamiliar music. The information in the chapters that follow will help you become familiar with the terminology required to answer the first question, and also apply it to the second question based on the set works.

This guide will help you to:

- Revise the key facts for each set work
- Practise writing essay answers that incorporate these key facts
- Improve the way you express your ideas.

Top tips

Keep listening to your prescribed works so that you begin to recognise and locate the key features covered in this guide. Remember also that, besides being able to analyse various musical works, you need to be able to present your arguments as clearly as possible; you may have to compare, contrast, assess, evaluate and comment as necessary.

Time management is a vital aspect of any exam. You are issued with a CD and can listen to the tests as many times as you like. This approach is intended to be helpful to you, but you must take care not to spend excessive amounts of time on one question at the expense of others. You should experiment with trial materials in order to find the optimum time you can allow for each question.

Perhaps as a starting-point, you may find it helpful to allow approximately:

- Ten minutes for each Section A listening test
- A further ten minutes for the dictation questions
- This will leave you with 50 minutes, which you could then divide into 20 minutes for essay 1 in Section B and 30 minutes for essay 2 in Section B.

Consider the following points:

- Take care not to stray from the question, because you may be penalised for irrelevance. (If the question asks for information about 'harmony', you won't get any marks for writing about melody)

- Keep referring to the terminology section, to be sure that you are focusing on the correct features of the music

- Do not worry if, sometimes, you seem to be stating the obvious! That is what examiners expect to see

- You don't need to include musical examples to gain full marks, and because you don't take a copy of the Anthology into the exam, you won't be expected to mention specific bar numbers. (However, try to be as precise as possible when describing specific sections of the music.)

- Keep listening to your set works, and following them in the Anthology

- You should write in continuous prose for both essays in Section B. If you begin to run out of time, however, use bullet points to ensure that everything you wish to say is included.

In addition to revision schemes, the final chapter of this guide provides examples of questions, indicative content (mark schemes) and specimen answers with commentaries for you to study.

FURTHER READING

- *Dictionary of Music in Sound* by David Bowman (ISBN 0-946890-87-0)
- *Writing about Music Workbook* by Alistair Wightman (RHG429)
- *Edexcel AS/A Level Music Study Guide 2016* by Hugh Benham and Alistair Wightman (RHG341)

Revision notes

Pages 17–71 provide a series of points that should help you to focus on the most important aspects of each set work. The 12 set works covered in this guide are divided into six sections corresponding to the areas of study

Edexcel has issued some guidance on how best to approach these examinations in a series of responses to frequently asked questions. They state at one point that students are expected to be 'familiar with the set works but are not expected to know each piece in depth'. But in response to a question about whether students need to reference bar and beats of the set works, they say that 'students should be aware of and be able to make reference to (where the question demands) the bar and beats of the set works in the Appraising exam'.

We suggest you try to develop an overview of each piece by checking that you understand the main points, using the terminology covered in the following chapter. After this, try to absorb some of the additional points, which will lead you to draw up examples that can be used to illustrate the work in question.

It is most important that you keep referring to the Anthology, and associate the points made in the lists that follow with what you hear in the music and read in the score. An attempt to learn these points in the form of abstract crib notes means you do not get anything out of the exercise long term, and run the risk of error.

Terminology

This section includes many of the terms you will need to know for your exam, but it is not exhaustive. You may not need to comment on all the points listed below for each and every set work.

Rhythm and metre

When writing about rhythm and metre, comment on:

- The variety of note lengths
- Recurring rhythmic patterns
- Dotted rhythms, or the 'reversed' dotted rhythm described as either a Scotch snap or Lombardic rhythm
- Syncopation
- Hemiola
- Triplets or other tuplets
- The time signature – whether it is simple or compound, duple, triple, quadruple or quintuple
- Metre changes
- Whether there is a metre at all.

Melody

When writing about melody, comment on:

- The range of the melody
- Whether it is in a major or minor key, or else modal or atonal
- Whether it is diatonic or chromatic

- The phrase structure – whether it is made up of balanced phrases ('periodic' phrasing) or something less regular
- Use of repetition or sequence
- Whether the melody is monotone (single note), conjunct (moving by step) or disjunct (moving by leap). If moving by leap, be ready to describe some of the intervals
- Use of motifs
- Whether the melody line is flowing or broken up by rests.

If you are describing vocal music, you will also be able to comment on aspects of text-setting:

- Whether the setting is syllabic (one note per syllable) or melismatic (several notes to a syllable)
- Whether verbal and musical accents coincide – in other words, whether the stressed syllables fall on the first beat or other strong beats of the bar, or not.

Harmony

You will be commenting on the music's vertical structure – the chords – and how they proceed from one to another. You may have to consider whether the chord is:

- A primary or secondary triad
- An augmented or diminished triad
- In root position or inverted
- Diatonic or chromatic
- Functional (broadly speaking, with cadential harmony that defines the key) or whether unrelated chords are used.

Other harmonic devices you may have to describe include:

- Cadences (perfect, imperfect/Phrygian, plagal, interrupted)
- Tonic or dominant pedals (specify which, and mention if the pedal is inverted)
- Circle of 5ths
- Tierce de Picardie.

You should also be prepared to comment on the presence of particular types of dissonance:

- Suspension
- False relation
- Appoggiatura
- 7th chords, or one of the higher dissonances (9th, 11th, 13th) – and also whether they are resolved

- Added 6th, augmented 6th, diminished 7th, Neapolitan 6th
- Added-note chords.

Tonality

Tonality is not another word for sound quality or timbre. It is about whether the music has a key, and you will have to be ready to consider the following points:

- Is the music tonal or atonal?
- If the music is tonal, is the harmony functional (with cadences that define the key)?
- Is the harmony non-functional? Perhaps the music still has a key signature, but is better regarded as being 'on' rather than 'in' the key?
- Some pieces might be modal – in which case, name the mode and the key it is based on. (Be careful: the music may not be modal throughout, or else may change modes as it goes on.)

> Remember that in tonality questions, you may have to associate a theme with its key to establish a location. Such references replace the use of bar numbers which would not be expected as you do not have access to the Anthology in the exam.

- In popular music, there are frequent pentatonic elements, and in these cases it is important to name the key as well – for example, E pentatonic major.
- Does the music modulate (change key systematically), as in most classical works, or does it abruptly 'shift' from one tonal centre to another?

Texture

This term applies to the way instruments/voices are combined to sound together, and also the number of parts involved. The number of parts will affect the density of the sound. Types of texture include:

> It is not enough at this level to describe a texture as 'thick' or 'thin'. You should aim, wherever possible, to state the number of parts, as well as the type of texture involved.

Monophonic	A single (unaccompanied) melody. (Note that a melody with a drone accompaniment is regarded as monophonic.)
Polyphonic	This term tends to be used as another way of saying contrapuntal – the combination of independently moving melody lines. It is generally better to reserve its use for early music, especially choral music of the Renaissance era.
Contrapuntal	See above. This term is freely applied in discussions of music from any period. The combination of independently moving lines may be: ■ Free: when there is no melodic similarity between the parts ■ Imitative: when another part enters with the same theme, while the first continues with its own music ■ Canonic: a strict form of imitation, when the second part is near enough an exact copy of the first, even if at a different pitch ■ Fugal: as in a fugue or fugato.

Do not confuse 'imitation' with repetition, antiphony or call-and-response.

If the passage is canonic, say whether the canon is at the octave, at the unison (the same pitch), at the 4th below, and so on. State, also, the length between the imitation – for example, two beats, one bar.

Make sure you can apply fugal terms, such as subject, answer, counter-subject, stretto, middle entry, codetta and so on.

| Homophony | ■ chordal textures, sometimes also described as homorhythmic: all parts having the same rhythm.
■ Melody-dominated homophony: textures in which the melody is supported by a rhythmically independent part – for example, Alberti bass or broken-chord patterns. You may prefer to use the expression 'melody and accompaniment'. |

Where the movement could be described as being in melody-dominated homophony, don't forget to mention transfers of the melody (for example from treble to bass), changes in accompanying patterns, and the numbers of parts (the density) used at any one time.

Heterophony	When a melody line is heard along with a rhythmically different or melodically varied version of itself.
Antiphony	When passages of music are performed by different singers and/or instrumentalists in alternation. The groups do not have to be evenly balanced.
	'Call-and-response' also refers to antiphony, particularly in jazz and popular music.

Other textural features include:

- Octaves – don't forget to say how many octaves there are, or to differentiate between octaves and unison
- Pedal points – also regarded as harmonic and tonal devices, although they have some bearing on the make-up of texture as well
- Ostinato – a short repeated melodic and/or rhythmic figure, heard in conjunction with other musical ideas. It also plays a prominent role in the overall texture
- Riff – a term for ostinato used in connection with jazz and popular music.

Performance forces and timbre

'Performance forces' simply means the voices and instruments used. You may also have to discuss methods of notation.

Timbre refers to the nature of the sound produced. Be ready to comment on the use of particular ranges (tessitura) of instruments or voices, as this may contribute to the overall sound created. For example, generally low sounds may be used to produce melancholy effects.

Also be ready to describe the effects of plucking and bowing, use of mutes, harmonics, and different bowing techniques, such as *sul ponticello*, *sul tasto*, or *sur la touche*.

Structure

Many questions will require you to comment on the structure or form of a given work. The most frequently encountered structural terms are as follows:

- Binary
- Rounded binary
- Ternary
- Fugue
- Sonata form

- Rondo
- Sonata rondo
- Variations
- Ritornello
- Through-composed

- Strophic
- Ground bass
- 12-bar blues
- Verse and refrain
- Tripartite.

Once you have identified the structure in general terms, be ready to give a more detailed description of the main sections in the music, giving changes of key and specific descriptive terms (e.g. first subject, exposition and so on).

Having identified the structure, avoid falling back on 'abstract' descriptions of the music. This can be a particular temptation in sonata form movements, but it is no use telling the examiner that there is an exposition with a first subject, transition and second subject without giving some information about keys and locations.

Historical context

You should be aware of the circumstances of composition and performance for each set work. It is also important to know how music from different eras, cultural and social backgrounds has developed with the passing of time.

With that in mind, you should collect information on the date and place of the first performance (where possible), and be clear who might have commissioned the music in the first place, the purpose of the music and the nature of the original audience. For example, if writing about sacred music, be ready to comment on the type of church and service, and when writing about jazz or popular music, bear in mind differences between live and studio performance.

In this guide, beats of the bar appear in superscript when part of a bar reference. For example, 'bar 4^3' means 'bar four, beat three'.

AREA OF STUDY 1:
Vocal music

Cantata 'Ein feste Burg ist unser Gott' BWV 80, 1st, 2nd and 8th movements (Bach)

Context

- A late-Baroque work, first performed on 31 October 1730 at St Thomas' Church in Leipzig where Bach was musical director. It was composed to mark the Festival of the Reformation – the celebration of Martin Luther's break with the Roman Catholic Church

- The Lutheran Cantata was performed before the sermon and reflected the subject of the day conveyed in the preceding reading (in this case Revelation 14, vs. 6–8)

- This type of cantata required vocal soloists, a small chorus, orchestra and continuo

- The full cantata is a multi-movement work, which – besides chorus, recitatives, arias and duets – includes a chorale for congregational use

- The text (in German) is taken from Martin Luther's hymn (known in English as 'A Stronghold Sure') for movements 1, 2, 5 and 8, and the remaining movements are settings of texts by Salomo Franck

- In the second movement, the chorale tune and text (soprano) are heard alongside Franck's poetry (bass).

Instrumental forces

- **Movement 1** is scored for four-part chorus (SATB), three oboes including: a taille (akin to cor anglais); strings consisting of violins I and II, viola, cello and violone (similar in range to double bass); and continuo instruments (organ and cembalo (harpsichord))

- Violins and viola double the soprano, alto and tenor lines, but the cello 'shadows' the bass, sometimes elaborating in heterophony

- **Movement 2** is a vocal duet for soprano and bass; the soprano doubled by oboe, sometimes in heterophony

- Violins I, II and violas provide an obbligato line in unison (a prominent and essential independent melody), supported by continuo

- **Movement 8**, the chorale, requires SATB with each part doubled by instruments: soprano and alto by oboe d'amore and violins; tenor by taille and viola; bass by continuo instruments.

Notation

- Various forms of traditional stave notation are employed
- Movement 1 has one stave for each instrument and vocal part, with cello and cembalo sharing a stave, and violone and organ allotted another
- In movement 2, violins and violas are combined on the one stave
- The chorale in movement 8 is laid out in open score, with indications regarding instrumentation at the start
- No dynamics are given, as is usual in Baroque music
- Harmonic content is indicated by figured bass, a form of musical shorthand in which each number below the bass line refers to an interval above.

> For further information on figured bass and the various symbols used, see *A2 Harmony Workbook* (Rhinegold Education, 2009) by Hugh Benham, pages 37–39.

Tempo, metre and rhythm

- No tempo indications are given, as performers were expected to rely on time signatures and the general character of the music to sense the speed
- Movement 1 is in a form of cut common time (¢), but in this case the score was laid out with four (rather than two) minims per bar. This type of time signature indicated a brisk pace
- Quadruple time was used for movements 2 and 8
- In movement 2, the 'moto perpetuo' semiquavers with walking bass quavers and florid shorter values in vocal parts and oboe necessitates a relatively fast but controlled tempo
- In movement 8, a more moderate tempo is required. The Bach chorale typically relies heavily on flowing quavers in the lower parts. Notice that the pause marks indicate ends of phrases rather than significant lengthening of notes.

Melody

- Luther's chorale provides the melodic basis of all three movements to be studied

- Movement 8 presents the chorale tune without elaboration. Notice its
  - Powerful repeated notes
  - Mainly conjunct movement with just the occasional leap
  - Forceful descending scale at end of first section and again in the final phrase
  - Single note outside the scale of D major (G♯)
- In movement 1, each phrase is presented in turn. There is a very loose variation of the chorale melody in the vocal parts, a direct statement of the theme being reserved for the oboes in canon with violone
- Heavy ornamentation of the chorale melody occurs in movement 2
- Other points to note:
  - Sequence, e.g. cello in bar 1, movement 1
  - Chromaticism, movement 1, bars 97–99; word painting to underline the guile of the devil
  - The mixture of syllabic word-setting and grouping of two or three notes per syllable in the chorale
  - The extended melismas in the choral writing of movement 1, and bass solo of movement 2
  - The angular, almost instrumental writing for the bass singer, e.g. movement 2, bars 13–18.

Harmony
- Bach's harmony is functional, with:
  - Clearly defined cadences
  - Triads and 7ths in various positions
  - Pedal points, e.g. movement 1, bar 27^3 to bar 30^3
  - Suspensions, e.g. a 4–3 suspension in movement 8, bar 2^2; 7–6 suspension in movement 8, bar 8^1; 9–8 suspension, movement 8, bar 10^2
  - Dissonances arising from freely moving lines and passing notes
  - Diminished 7ths, e.g. movement 1, bar 71^{1-2}.

Tonality
- In movement 1, the chorale dominates throughout, meaning that the chorale's key (D major) is of major structural importance
- For variety, however, other related keys are employed, for example:
  - E minor (bars 63–64)

- B minor (bars 65–66)
- F♯ minor (bars 67–68)
- A major (bar 90)

- In movement 2, also in D major, there are again modulations to closely related keys, e.g. A major (bar 27), B minor (bar 46)
- Movement 8 provides insights into Bach's ingenious handling of a theme that could have been largely harmonised in D, e.g. perfect cadences in A major (bars 5 and 9) and imperfect cadence in E minor (bar 10).

Structure

Structures in the three prescribed movements are dictated by the chorale melody.

- Movement 1 takes each phrase in turn and presents it first in a fugal working-out in the vocal parts before rounding it off with a canonic version for oboes and violone
- Movement 2 uses ritornello form, i.e. a theme recurs at various points throughout the movement (upper strings), sometimes touching on different keys. Imposed on this scheme are statements of the chorale (soprano) with a different 'parallel' text in the bass
- Movement 8: a nine-line chorale, with repetitions (e.g. phrase 4 uses the same music as phrase 2, and phrase 9 has the same melodic line).

Texture

- Movement 1 is contrapuntal, with imitative writing in the vocal parts in fugal style, and canon at the octave in oboes and violone, with a half-bar between the entries
- The texture is further complicated by the heterophony in the cello at bars 20–22, where it plays a more elaborate version of the vocal bass line
- Movement 2 is also contrapuntal with a ritornello theme in upper strings, supported by a walking bass, over which can be heard an embellished version of the chorale in the soprano (with heterophony in the oboe part) and an independent line in the solo bass part
- Movement 8 is homophonic, though the lower parts are rhythmically independent.

FURTHER LISTENING

Listen to other works by Bach, e.g. the Brandenburg Concertos, Cantata No. 140, 'Wachet auf!', and also cantatas of a later period, such as Britten's St. Nicolas.

Die Zauberflöte, No. 4 (recit and aria: 'O zittre nicht') and No. 5 (quintet: 'Hm! Hm! Hm! Hm!) from Act 1 (Mozart)

Context

- This work is an example of a Classical-period opera
- *The Magic Flute (Die Zauberflöte)* is a Singspiel, a type of German language opera with spoken dialogue in place of the recitative that separates the arias, ensemble numbers and choruses in other types of opera. Recitative, which appears in No. 4, was reserved for the more dramatic moments
- First performed on 30 September, 1791
- It is a fantastical tale incorporating the ideals of the 18th century Enlightenment and Freemasonry
- It requires vocal soloists, chorus (though not in the prescribed extracts) and orchestra.

In No. 4, The Queen of the Night commands the hero, Tamino, to rescue her daughter, Pamina, from the clutches of the (supposed) villain, Sarastro. In No. 5, Papageno provides comic relief as he struggles with a gag placed on him by the Queen's attendants, the Three Ladies, as a punishment for lying. After he is freed, Tamino and Papageno are sent on their quest to rescue Pamina, protected respectively by a magic flute and bells, and guided by the Three Boys.

Sonority

- The soloists in these pieces are:
    - The Queen of the Night, sung by a high (coloratura) soprano
    - Tamino, a tenor
    - Papageno, a baritone
    - The Three Ladies, all of them soprano. They have separate parts, heard in homophony – though at bar 237, the first and second sopranos double at the unison
- Only part of the orchestra is required in these pieces: two oboes, two bassoons, two horns in B♭, and strings in No. 4, and the same forces plus clarinets in No. 5
- Pizzicato is used in the Andante in No. 5, bar 214 onwards.

Notation

- The music is presented as a vocal score with individual lines for each vocalist with the exception of the 1st and 2nd Ladies, whose parts are printed on the same stave
- Italian terms are used for tempos, even though the work uses the German language.

> Use of German for tempo indications was only introduced by Beethoven in his later works, in which both Italian and German directions are given.

- The usual (Italian) dynamic indications are used, though only rarely in the vocal parts (e.g. No. 5, bars 192–203)
- The direction 'sotto voce' ('under the voice') is used for the Three Ladies at bar 184 in No. 5
- In this score, German terms and abbreviations are used for the instruments, some of the less obvious terms are:
  - Br. for Bratsche (viola)
  - Bläs. for Bläser (wind instruments).

Tempo, metre and rhythm

- Both numbers contain tempo contrasts:
  - No. 4: Allegro maestoso – Larghetto – Allegro moderato
  - No. 5: Allegro – Moderato
- Metres also change:
  - No.4: simple quadruple ($\frac{4}{4}$) for the two allegro sections, contrasting with simple triple ($\frac{3}{4}$) in the Larghetto
  - No. 5: 'Cut common time' (fast two minims per bar) changing to more relaxed quadruple ($\frac{4}{4}$) in the Moderato
- Notice the following rhythmic features:
  - Syncopation in the orchestral introduction of No. 4, imparting a sense of urgency
  - The 'free time' delivery in the recitative section
  - Frequent dotted rhythms
  - Rapid, dramatic flourishes, e.g. the triplet semiquavers in the Allegro moderato (No. 4, bars 62–63)

- Virtuoso streams of semiquavers (No. 4, bars 79–92)
- Insertion of rests within melody of Andante (No. 5, bars 218–219).

Melody

- Overall the vocal range of 'The Queen of the Night's recitative and aria is wide, from D just above middle C, to F two octaves and a 3rd higher
- The last bar of the No. 4 Recitative contains a falling diminished 7th and a typical closing formula for recitatives, i.e. the falling 4th (see music example below)
- Unusual phrase structure at the start of the aria in No. 4, consisting of 3+3+2+2 bars
- Ornamentation and appoggiaturas intensify expressive power
- Sequence (No. 4, bars 28–31)
- Chromatic descent (No. 4, bars 41–43) for pathos
- Melody in the No. 4 Allegro moderato frequently contains rapidly moving scales
- Word-setting involves a mix of syllabic, slurred quavers and melismas
- Melody in the Quintet, No. 5 is marked by:
  - Periodic phrasing
  - Generally diatonic writing
  - Repeated notes.

Harmony

- Functional, with clearly defined perfect and imperfect cadences
- Interrupted cadences also appear, e.g. No. 4 bars 55–56
- Neapolitan 6th (No. 4, bar 19), followed by
- Diminished 7th (No. 4, bar 20)

No. 4, bars 18-21

- Tonic pedal at opening of No. 4
- Appoggiatura chord is used at bar 52 of No. 4
- Suspensions are rare, but see No. 4, bar 66[1]
- Notice the Augmented 6th chord in No. 5 at bar 150.

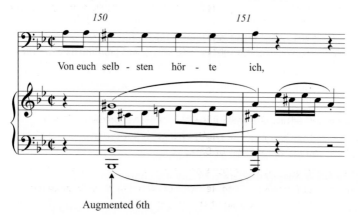

Augmented 6th

Tonality

- Both numbers are in the key of B♭ major and modulate to related keys, e.g.
  - G minor (No. 4, bar 21)
  - C minor (No. 4, bar 38)
  - F major (No. 5, bar 34)
  - D minor (No. 5, bar 142)
  - E flat (No. 5, bar 172)

The five related keys in this instance are the dominant (F), subdominant (E♭), relative minor (G minor), and relative minors of the dominant (D minor) and subdominant (C minor).

Structure

- No. 4 is a recitative and aria
- In this case the recitative is orchestrally accompanied.

> Normally, dialogue in Singspiel was spoken, but accompanied recitative was sometimes used for scenes requiring heightened expression.

- The aria is in two sections, reflecting the developing dramatic situation:
  - Largo, in which the Queen of the Night expresses sorrow at the loss of her daughter and condemnation of Sarastro
  - Allegro moderato, in which Tamino is commanded to rescue Pamina
- No. 5 is a through-composed ensemble number with clearly differentiated sections that also reflect the course of the action.

Texture

- Mainly melody-dominated homophony (melody with accompaniment)
- Homophony (homorhythm), e.g. No. 5, bars 74–77
- Octaves, e.g. No. 5, bars 61–64.

FURTHER LISTENING

Beethoven's *Fidelio* and Weber's *Der Freischütz* are both examples of Singspiel. For an example of opera in which all sections are sung, see Mozart's *Marriage of Figaro* or *Don Giovanni*.

AREA OF STUDY 2:
Instrumental music

Concerto in D minor Op. 3 No. 11 RV 565 (Vivaldi)

Context
- Late Baroque
- Concerto grosso: a work for a group of soloists (concertino) – in this case two violins and a cello – supported by a group of string players and harpsichord/organ continuo
- Vivaldi was an Italian (Venetian) composer. This work was published in Amsterdam in 1711 as one of the 12 concertos that form *L'estro Armonico* ('*Harmonic Fancy*' or '*Harmonic Inspiration*')
- The exact date of composition cannot be established and it might have been much earlier than the date of publication.

Sonority and performance forces
- Three solo strings with a larger accompanying group including continuo – a 'cembalo' (harpsichord) and a violone (equivalent of a double bass)
- The strings are bowed throughout
- Violin range extends up to D, just over two octaves above middle C
- Solo cello extends to G above middle C
- Resonant exploitation of open strings at the start of the work
- Contrast of forces plays an essential part throughout
- The central part of the slow (third) movement (Largo e spiccato) is for upper strings only; the bass instruments and continuo rest at this point.

Note that contrasts in performing forces had played a major role in Venetian music for over a century before Vivaldi. See works by Giovanni Gabrieli and Claudio Monteverdi.

Notation

- The version printed in the Anthology is a full score with each part allotted its own line
- The Anthology score does not differentiate between soloists and ripieno, but Violins I and II are soloists, and III and IV are ripieno. The solo cello line is on the stave above the continuo
- Typical Baroque features of the score include:
  - Figured bass – a system of harmonic shorthand, which conveyed to the keyboard player the chords to be supplied. Figures indicate the intervals above the bass. The indication 'Tasto solo' (see movement 2, bar 58) means that only the bass line, without chords, is to be played at this point
  - Dynamics are 'terraced' – bold, abrupt contrasts between loud and soft. There are no crescendo or diminuendo marks; mid-volume dynamics, such as $\boldsymbol{mp}$ and $\boldsymbol{mf}$, are avoided
  - Italian indications are performance instructions, e.g. *spiccato* (detached bow strokes).

Tempo, metre and rhythm

Tempo

- According to the Anthology, the concerto consists of four main sections: Allegro – brief 'Adagio e spiccato' leading to Allegro – Largo e spiccato – Allegro

Metre

- The first movement (Allegro) is in $\frac{3}{4}$
- The second movement (Adagio e spiccato; Allegro) is in common time in both sections
- The third movement (Largo e spiccato) is in compound quadruple ($\frac{12}{8}$) time
- The fourth movement – Allegro – returns to common time.

Rhythm

- Movements I, II and IV are characterised by typically Baroque 'motor' rhythms, i.e. hard-driven patterns, helped along by the almost percusive harpsichord continuo
- Movement I opens with continuous quavers, leading to running semiquavers
- The short Adagio section at the start of movement II is rhythmically simple with four even quavers followed by a minim with pause
- Movement III draws on rocking Siciliano rhythms.

Melody

- Broken chord patterns in opening bars of first movement (I)
- Scales (descending at II, bar 13, and inverted to rise at II, bar 37)
- Sequences are frequent, e.g. II, bars 25–26
- Leaps, e.g. 5ths at II, bars 25–26 and 7th at III, bar 4
- Chromatic, e.g. IV, bars 4-6
- Ornaments are confined to the occasional trill.

Harmony

- Functional, with strong drive to cadences
- Vocabulary draws on root position chords, first inversions and 7ths
- Frequent circles of 5ths (II, bars 33–35)
- Suspensions, e.g. 4–3 at II, bar 50
- An unusual false relation occurs at II, bar 3 (i.e. E♭ in C minor chord followed by E♮ in a different part of the succeeding A major chord)
- Neapolitan 6th chord, e.g. III, bar 2^2
- Diminished 7th, III, bar 5^2
- Dominant pedal at II, bars 58–69.

Tonality

- Vivaldi uses a tonal scheme based on functional harmonies, defined by cadences
- This system of functional tonality allows modulations
- The tonic key of all three movements is D minor
- Vivaldi modulates mainly to related keys:
    - A minor (II, bar 32)
    - G minor (II, bar 48)
    - F major (II, bar 52)
- Unusually, Vivaldi moves to the unrelated key of F minor in III, bars 7–8
- Other devices used to underline tonality include:
    - Circle of 5ths progressions (e.g. II, bars 33–35)
    - Dominant pedal (see bars 58–69 at end of the second movement)
    - Tierce de Picardie (II, bar 70), which unusually leads to a conclusion in the tonic minor.

Structure

- Movement I: bars 1–31
- Movement II: introductory Adagio (bars 1–3) leading to Allegro (bars 4–73)
  - In the allegro starting at bar 4, fugal textures are coordinated within a scheme of contrasting tutti-solo sections
  - Though not a complete fugue, it is appropriate to use fugal terminology in describing the start of the Allegro:
  - Subject – the theme announced in the bass in the tonic at bar 4
  - Answer – the second entry of the theme, now in the dominant (viola at bar 8)
  - Countersubject – the 'countermelody' to the answer in the bass at bar 8
  - Countersubject 2 – an additional counterpoint to both subject and counter-subject (bass, bar 12)
- Movement III is in ternary form (A–B–A)
- Movement IV is in a loose ritornello form. The recurring ritornello theme embraces both solo and tutti sections, and is identifiable by reference to motifs at bars 1, 7 and 11.

The basic outline of the movement is as follows:

Bar 1	Ritornello	D minor
Bar 14	Episode	
Bar 19	Ritornello	A minor
Bar 30	Episode	
Bar 53	Ritornello (shortened)	D minor
Bar 59	Episode	
Bar 68	Ritornello (final motif)	D minor

Texture

- Movement I opens with a two-part canon at the distance of a crotchet beat, lengthening at bar 6 to a bar between imitations. The passage at bar 20 is a cello melody with continuo accompaniment
- The Adagio at the start of movement II is homophonic
- The Allegro from bar 4 of movement II is fugal
- Movement III is melody-dominated homophony, with lower strings and continuo omitted in the central section
- Movement IV is contrapuntal at the opening, but other passages are more homophonic. In these sections, notice the differentiation between accompaniments of crotchet chords followed by crotchet rest (bar 7) and those with continuous quavers (bar 36).

FURTHER LISTENING

You could refer to other Baroque composers of concerti grossi, e.g. Corelli, Handel and J. S. Bach. In more recent times, comparisons could be drawn with Stravinsky (*Dumbarton Oaks*) and Tippett (Concerto for Double String Orchestra).

Clara Schumann, Piano Trio in G minor, Op. 17: movement 1

Context

- Romantic era work, completed in 1846
- A piano trio is a chamber work with parts for violin, cello and piano, popularised by Haydn and taken up by composers such as Mozart, Beethoven, Brahms and Shostakovich
- This trio has four movements, but you are only required to study the first movement
- Clara Schumann: daughter of Friedrich Wieck, a celebrated piano teacher; wife of composer Robert Schumann. She was one of a limited number of 19th-century women composers, other near contemporaries being Fanny Mendelssohn, sister of composer Felix Mendelssohn, and Maria Szymanowska.

Sonority

- All three instruments are treated in a conventional manner
- Ranges are well within each instrument's capabilities: nearly three octaves for violin and cello, and five and a half octaves for piano
- Limited use of pizzicato in cello, e.g. bars 238–246
- Double-stopping in violin, e.g. bars 21–23
- Piano pedalling indications are rare.

Notation

- The two stringed instruments are allotted a stave each, their parts printed above the piano's two staves
- When leaving the lower ranges, notated in bass clef, the cello part is printed in treble clef (not tenor), sounding an octave lower than written (see bar 122)
- Dynamics range between *ff* and *p*, with frequent use of crescendos and diminuendos
- Tempo indications are Italian.

Tempo, metre and rhythm

Tempo

- Allegro moderato, though the metronome mark of 152 crotchets per minute is relatively brisk
- Changes in tempo are rare, notably 'poco rit.' (bar 56 and 220), although the 'animato' at bar 266 invites an increase of pace to approach the end

Metre

- Common time throughout

Rhythm

- Persistent quaver movement
- Syncopation (e.g. bars 39–40)
- Forceful dotted rhythms.

Melody

- Balanced phrases
- Sequential repetition (e.g. bars 14–17)
- Melodic leaps in the violin part include: augmented 4th (bar 25), minor 6th (bar 29), minor 7th (bars 29–30)

- Opening violin melody is marked by strong perfect 5ths (bar 1) and leap of an octave (bar 6)
- Use of appoggiatura to intensify expressive effect (e.g. bar 7^1, violin)
- Chromaticism (e.g. strings, bars 66–67).

Harmony

- Clara Schumann's harmony is functional and marked by a strong drive towards cadences:
  - Imperfect, bar 4
  - Perfect, bars 21–22
  - Plagal, bars 285–286
- Suspensions, e.g. bar 18
- Chromatic chords:
  - Neapolitan 6th (bar 191)
  - Diminished 7th (bar 13^2)
  - French augmented 6th (bar 11^4)
- Anticipation (bar 5^4, violin)
- Dominant pedal (bars 155–164, cello).

Structure and tonality

The movement is in sonata form and for the most part modulates to related keys:

Exposition (repeated) bars 1–90		
Bars 1–21	1st subject	G minor
Bars 22–45	Bridge	
Bars 45–85	2nd subject	B♭ major
Bars 85–90	Codetta	Transitioning back to G minor

Development bars 91–164 (based largely on 1st subject)		
C minor (bar 92–94)		
E♭ (bar 107)		
F minor (bar 111)		
C minor (from bar 127)		
G minor (from bar 150) with dominant pedal from bar 155		

Recapitulation bars 165–249		
Bars 165–185	1st subject	G minor
Bars 186–210	Bridge	
Bars 210–249	2nd subject	G major
Bars 250–288	Coda	G minor

Texture

- Mainly homophonic (e.g. bars 21–23) or melody-dominated homophony (e.g. bars 1–8)
- Some contrapuntal exchanges between violin and cello, from bar 115
- Melodic interest is usually kept in the violin or right hand of piano
- Cello reinforces violin line in octaves (bar 47) or in 10ths (from bar 17)
- Piano part is often made up of broken chords (maintaining a flow of quavers) or is chordal (bar 41).

FURTHER LISTENING

Useful comparisons could be made with works by Beethoven (Archduke Trio), Brahms (Piano Trio No. 3), Dvořák (Dumky Trio) and Shostakovich (Piano Trio No. 2).

AREA OF STUDY 3:
Music for film

'The Duchess' (Opening and End titles), 'Mistake of Your Life', 'Six Years Later' and 'Never See Your Children Again', from *The Duchess* (2008) (Rachel Portman)

Context

- *The Duchess* was released in 2008 and is based on the life of Georgina Cavendish, Duchess of Devonshire (1757–1806), her unhappy marriage, and affair with Charles Grey, 2nd Earl Grey
- The score is by Rachel Portman (b. 1960); her other film scores include *Chocolat* (2000) and *The Manchurian Candidate* (2004)
- Portman's scores avoid electronic and synthesised sound effects
- The score of *The Duchess* is made up of 18 cues, two of which are taken directly from classical sources (Beethoven's German Dance No. 10 and the Adagio from Haydn's String Quartet, Op. 1, No. 3)
- Classical pastiche is avoided in the cues, which Portman composed, in favour of a generally delicate underscore
- Two of the prescribed cues ('Mistake of Your Life' and 'Never See Your Children Again') effectively help to create a bleaker mood.

Notation

- The cues are notated in the form of orchestral short scores. The music is compressed for the most part on to two staves at a time with instrumentation indicated as required
- Tempo is indicated by metronome marks with occasional use of Italian terms
- Instrument names are given in English, although some Italian terminology is employed (tacet, tutti)
- Traditional dynamics marks are used.

Sonority

- Portman uses a relatively small orchestra, consisting of strings, woodwind, horns, harp and timpani

- Instruments are treated in a conventional manner, with some use of string pizzicato (e.g. 'Six Years Later')
- A violin solo can be heard in the first cue ('The Duchess' (Opening), bar 17)
- Effective use is made of solo timpani in 'Mistake of Your Life'.

Texture

- Melody-dominated homophony is used in all the prescribed cues, but notice:
  - Pedal in the Opening (bars 17–36)
  - Dominant pedal with timpani rhythm in 'Mistake of Your Life'
  - Waltz patterns in 'Six Years Later'
  - Thinning out of texture at the close of 'Six Years Later'.

Tempo, metre and rhythm

Tempo

- Moderately fast for the Opening and End Titles
- Brisk waltz time for 'Six Years Later'
- Slow for 'Mistake of Your Life' and 'Never See Your Children Again'

Metre

- Quadruple for Opening and End Titles, and second part of 'Six Years Later'
- Compound duple ($\frac{6}{8}$) for first part of 'Six Years Later' with two bars of triple-time waltz for each $\frac{6}{8}$ bar
- Triple time for 'Mistake of Your Life' and 'Never See Your Children Again'

Rhythm

- Continuous quavers in both fast and slow movements
- Syncopation in the Opening (see accompaniment in bar 1 and melody in bar 10)
- Occasional triplets in the Opening (e.g. bar 22)
- Ominous timpani pattern in both 'Mistake of Your Life' (shown below) and 'Never See Your Children Again'

- Long sustained notes in 'Never See Your Children Again'.

Melody

- There is some use of modality, e.g. the melody of the Opening is in D major, but there are mixolydian inflections, e.g. the C♮ in bar 7
- In all cues, there is frequent step movement, sometimes interspersed with leaps of 3rd, 4th, 6th (e.g. in the Opening)
- Other features include:
  - Appoggiaturas (e.g. bar 18 of the Opening)
  - Auxiliary notes (e.g. bars 2 and 35 of the Opening)
  - Sequential repetition (e.g. 'Mistake of Your Life', bar 27, where the preceding eight-bar phrase in G minor is repeated a tone higher in A minor)
  - Expressive minor 6ths (e.g. 'Mistake of your life', piano bars 35–38):

  - Melody formed from broken chords, in bars 3–6 of 'Six Years Later':

Harmony

- Harmony is broadly functional with perfect cadences (e.g. the Opening, bars 13–16)
- Harmonic rhythm (i.e. rate of chord change) is generally slow
- Modal elements are evident, with the frequent use of a 'modal' dominant chord, i.e. where the leading note is lowered a semitone so that in place of an A major chord, an A minor chord is used in the Opening and End Titles, while in 'Mistake of Your Life', a D minor chord replaces D major in the key of G minor
- Other devices include:
  - Use of unprepared and unresolved 7ths, e.g. the Opening, bar 11
  - Pedal points, e.g. tonic (the Opening, bars 17–36) and dominant ('Mistake of your life', bars 1–18)
  - Internal pedal ('Never See Your Children Again', bars 7–25)
  - Harmonic sequences ('Mistake of Your Life', bars 19–34)
  - Open 5th chords ('Mistake of Your Life', bar 73)
  - Unstable second inversion for final cadence ('Mistake of Your Life', bars 81–82)
  - Augmented triad ('Six Years Later', bars 25 and 27)

- Diminished triad (bars 34–37) and unprepared dissonances (e.g. added E against the opening pedal D) in 'Never See Your Children Again'
- Variation of basic vocabulary in 'End Titles' through the addition of chords of F major, G major (first inversion) and E min7.

Tonality

- Tonality of the Opening, 'Six Years Later' and End Titles is D mixolydian. The C♯, which would have occurred in a major scale, is replaced with a C♮. These three cues have no modulation
- The key of 'Mistake of Your Life' is G minor, with both modal and ordinary 'functional' dominant chords
- In 'Mistake of Your Life', there are brief excursions to A minor
- 'Never See Your Children Again' is in a non-functional D minor.

Structure

- This score is less concerned with matching specific images to the course of the music than the creation of a more generally expressive underscore. Consequently there are clear traces of formal musical organisation and symmetry, as well as the reprising of large parts of already announced material, e.g. the repetitions of music from the Opening in the second section of 'Six years later' and the modified repetitions in the End Titles.

- The Opening consists of three separate themes heard one after another and without development:

Bars 1–16

Bars 17–34

Bars 35-43: motif **X** is also extended in the End Titles   **X**

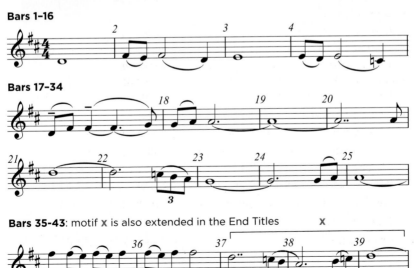

■ 'Mistake of Your Life' consists of an introduction followed by two themes heard in alternation. These themes share a resemblance with motifs from the Opening. (Compare bars 17–34 on page 37 with the first theme of this cue):

■ 'Six Years Later' is in two sections: first a 'waltz', which in harmonic content (tonic–'modal' dominant) relates to the Opening; and secondly a substantial reprise of music from the Opening.

■ 'Never See Your Children Again' is more atmospheric, and is through-composed

■ 'End titles' largely follows the course of the Opening, although one motif in particular (marked **x** on page 37) is subjected to more development, and the harmonic vocabulary is expanded to take in additional chords.

Main theme ('Birth of a Penguin Part II'), 'Birth of a Penguin Part 1', 'Rise and Fall from Grace' and 'Batman vs the Circus', from *Batman Returns* (1992) (Danny Elfman)

Context

■ The *Batman* films are fantasies based on the comic-book character Batman, and his encounters with ingenious criminals, in this case the Penguin and Catwoman

■ *Batman Returns* was directed by Tim Burton, and is a sequel to his *Batman* (1989)

■ The score was provided by Danny Elfman (b.1953), composer of incidental music for film and TV, perhaps most famously for *The Simpsons*

■ The score is popular and direct in style, with vivid, grand orchestral effects

■ Much of the orchestration was undertaken by Steve Bartek, aided by Mark McKenzie

■ Elfman uses a leitmotif system, with clearly defined themes for each character.

The term Leitmotif was first used in connection with the operas of Wagner, where motifs were used to represent the characters and also objects (e.g. swords) and concepts (e.g. love, grief). In the course of his operas such motifs were subjected to development and transformation as the changing situation demanded, and a similar process occurs in Elfman's score.

Notation

- The cues are notated in the form of orchestral short scores. The music is compressed onto varying numbers of staves, ranging from two or three up to nine in 'Batman vs the Circus', with instrumentation and vocal parts indicated as required.

'Cue' is the term used to indicate the music used for a particular point or scene in the film.

Sonority

Elfman draws on a full symphony orchestra, and the following additional instruments:

- Organ
- A children's choir
- Synthesiser
- Celeste
- Piano
- Accordion
- Large percussion section, including xylophone, marimba, temple blocks, sleighbells, tam-tam, cymbals

Colouristic effects include:

- Strings – tremolandi, pizzicato, glissandi
- Woodwinds – flutter-tongue (flute); wide vibrato (oboe)
- Brass – use of mutes, horn glissando
- Choir – vocalisation.

Texture

Textures are generally homophonic:

- Chordal ('Birth of a Penguin Part I', bar 14)
- Melody-dominated homophony ('Birth of a Penguin Part II', bar 27 onwards – this is the Batman motif)
- Layered ostinati (opening of 'Birth of a Penguin Part II')
- Octaves ('Birth of a Penguin Part I', bars 22–25)
- High pitch string clusters ('The Rise and Fall from Grace', bars 7–8)
- Waltz rhythm with sustained octaves in bass ('Rise and Fall', bars 20–25)
- Pedal ('Birth of a Penguin Part II', bars 85–92).

Tempo, metres and rhythm

Tempo

- Indicated by metronome marks
- Most of the cues are moderate in pace, though 'Batman vs the Circus' moves from slow to very fast.

Metre

- There are occasional changes of time signature, e.g. one bar of $\frac{3}{8}$ at bar 13 of 'Birth of a Penguin Part I', and the insertion of the waltz episode (bars 20–25) within a mainly quadruple time context for 'Rise and Fall from Grace'.

Rhythm

- Notable **rhythmic** features include:
  - Pounding triplets in the Batman theme and its accompaniment ('Birth of a Penguin Part II', bar 25 onwards)
  - Loose augmentations, e.g. bar 65 of 'Birth of a Penguin Part II'
  - Almost constant quavers in 'Batman vs the Circus'.

Melody

- The two most important leitmotifs are:

  - The Batman motif and its variants:

Birth of a Penguin Part I, bar 1

Birth of a Penguin Part II, bar 27

  - Motifs associated with the Penguin, first of which is a four-note idea:

Birth of a Penguin Part I, bar 3

- The second motif appears briefly in the course of the opening cue, but can be heard most clearly in 'Rise and Fall from Grace'

Rise and Fall from Grace, bars 8-11

- Fragmentary melodic lines occur in 'Batman vs the Circus' (oboe at bars 57–58, the fairground steam organ at bars 62–63)
- The first of the Penguin motifs occurs as part of a quaver 'moto perpetuo' in 'Batman vs the Circus', bars 26–27. Notice the first of each four-quaver group:

Batman versus the Circus, bars 26-27

Harmony

- Functional language, with frequent cadences
- Tonic pedals (e.g. 'Birth of a Penguin Part II', bars 1–8)
- Diminished triads (e.g. 'Birth of a Penguin Part I', bar 34^3)
- Diminished 7th ('Birth of a Penguin Part I', bar 37^2)
- Augmented triad ('Rise and Fall from Grace', bar 51)
- False relations ('Birth of a Penguin Part II', bars 93–96)
- Added 6th chords ('Batman vs the Circus', bar 5)
- Neapolitan harmony ('Rise and Fall from Grace', bar 45)
- Whole-tone chords ('Rise and Fall from Grace', bars 50–52).

Structure and tonality

- All the prescribed cues are through-composed, drawing on the various leitmotifs, as and when the film action requires
- Keys are clearly defined by cadences and sometimes by pedals
- Tonality is not structurally significant. For example, 'Birth of a Penguin Part I' opens in B♭ minor and closes in D minor, 'Birth of a Penguin Part II' continues in D minor and finishes in C♯ minor
- 'Batman versus the Circus' opens in B minor and closes in E minor
- 'Rise and Fall from Grace' is the only one of the prescribed cues to remain anchored to a single tonality (C minor – C major)
- Key changes are often sudden, e.g. 'Birth of a Penguin Part I' moves from F minor (bars 3–6), A minor (bars 7–10) and then to G minor (bars 11–13)
- Key changes sometimes involve keys unrelated to one another, e.g. 'Birth of a Penguin Part I', bars 26–31 in D minor to bars 32–33 in F♯ minor and then bars 34–37 in G minor
- Sense of key is occasionally weakened by use of whole-tone structures, e.g. bars 50–52 in 'Rise and Fall from Grace'.

AREA OF STUDY 4:
Popular music and jazz

'Lady Day and (John Coltrane)', 'Inner State (of Mind)' and 'Love and Affection', from *Back in the Day* (2000) (Courtney Pine)

Context

- Courtney Pine (b.1964) is a contemporary jazz musician, whose style blends soul, rhythm and blues, reggae, and hip hop with traditional elements
- He is a virtuoso saxophonist, who also performs on flute, bass clarinet and keyboards
- *Back in the Day* (issued in 2000) was Pine's eighth album, one which he produced himself
- Three of the album's 15 tracks are prescribed for study, and two of these are cover versions: 'Lady Day and (John Coltrane)' by Gil Scott-Heron (1971) and 'Love and affection' by Joan Armatrading (1976).

Notation

- The Anthology shows a short score with piano, vocal, and chord symbols with guitar tab above the stave. Other instrumental parts are notated on an additional stave, as required
- Cross-heads are used to indicate the rhythms in the rap sections as well as multiphonics and key-click effects
- Dynamics are shown in a traditional manner
- Tempo is given as beats per minute
- Occasionally, other effects are written into the score, e.g. vibrato, bar 39.

Sonority

There is a considerable contrast of instruments used between the three songs:

- 'Lady Day and (John Coltrane)' is scored for vocals, piano, guitars and saxophone
- 'Inner State (of Mind)' draws on the so-called 'jazz horn' grouping, which confusingly does not include horns but instead saxophone, trumpet and trombone. Other resources include vocals, rap and guitars
- 'Love and affection' includes vocal, bvox, guitar, bass clarinet, tenor sax and strings.

Notice the following features:

- Distortions and random background sounds at start of 'Inner State (of Mind)'
- Dubbed voices in 'Inner State (of Mind)' and 'Lady Day and (John Coltrane)'
- Use of what the CD sleeve notes call a 'drum programme' in 'Inner State (of Mind)' and 'Lady Day and (John Coltrane)'
- Extended performance techniques (multiphonics and key clicks) in 'Lady Day and (John Coltrane)'
- Variation of vocal timbres in 'Love and affection'.

Texture

The predominant texture is homophony or melody-dominated homophony. See table below for locations of various features:

Texture	'Inner State (of Mind)'	'Lady Day and (John Coltrane)'	'Love and affection'
Homophonic	Voices (bar 1) Horns and sax (bars 70-71)	Close harmony (bar 21)	
Melody-dominated homophony	e.g. bars 2-9 (sax and piano)	Bar 1 onwards	Bars 1-12
Rap with accompaniment	e.g. bars 21-35		

Broken chords	Bars 80–87 (RH piano)		
Riff	e.g. bars 94–115	e.g. bars 5–12	e.g. bars 22 onwards
Free counterpoint			Bars 84–94

Tempo, metre and rhythm

- 'Inner State (of Mind)' is in a brisk quadruple metre throughout
- 'Lady Day and (John Coltrane)' moves from fast quadruple to a slower rubato section at the close
- 'Love and Affection' opens with a rubato quadruple time passage, before moving into an upbeat strict tempo.

Rhythmic features are located in the table below. (There are many other instances of some of these, which you might find it helpful to write in):

Rhythmic features	'Inner state (of mind)'	'Lady Day and (John Coltrane)'	'Love and affection'
Syncopation	e.g. bars 2 and 3		
Dotted rhythm	Bar 11	Bar 81	
Scotch snap	Bar 75	Bar 31	
Triplets		Bar 126	Bar 25
Irregular groupings	Bar 97		Bar 31

Long sustained notes		Bars 46–48	
Off-beat chords			Bars 13–14
Cross-rhythms			Bar 12 ('really laugh')

Melody

The prescribed songs are typically characterised by:

- Pentatonicism (e.g. 'Inner State (of Mind)', bars 1–2; 'Love and Affection' strings motif uses minor pentatonic scale, bars 84–85)
- Blue notes (e.g. 'Inner State (of Mind)', bar 2, G♭; 'Lady Day and (John Coltrane), bar 23, G♭)
- Chromaticism (e.g. 'Inner State (of Mind)', bar 100, note the ornamented chromatic descent C–B–B♭–A; 'Lady Day', bar 75; 'Love and Affection', bass clarinet, bars 30–32).

Other noteworthy features include:

- Borrowing of melody from Gershwin's 'Summertime' from *Porgy and Bess* in 'Inner State (of Mind)'
- Scat singing ('Inner State (of Mind)', bars 52–53)
- Melismas ('Love and Affection', bar 47)
- Conjunct lines ('Love and Affection', bars 16–19)
- Narrow-range lines ('Lady Day and (John Coltrane)', bars 5–7)
- Repetition of short figures ('Inner state (of Mind), bar 99)
- Frequent ornamentation, e.g. in 'Lady Day and (John Coltrane)':
  - Acciaccaturas (bar 8)
  - Controlled vibrato (bar 39)
  - Bending of notes (bar 45)
  - Fall-offs (bar 50)
  - Sliding up to pitch (bar 52)
  - Glissandos (bar 55).

Harmony

- 12-bar blues ('Lady Day and (John Coltrane)')
- 7th chords ('Lady Day and (John Coltrane)', bar 21)
- 7ths are sometimes laced with ♯9ths, which produce false relations ('Lady Day and (John Coltrane)', bar 1)
- 9th chords ('Lady Day and (John Coltrane)', bar 47)
- 13th chords ('Lady Day and (John Coltrane)', bar 81)
- Some quartal harmony ('Inner State (of Mind)', bars 70–71)
- False relations ('Inner State (of Mind)', bar 18)
- Half-diminished chords ('Inner state (of Mind)', bar 53³)
- Augmented chord ('Lady Day and (John Coltrane)', bar 119)
- Parallel harmony ('Lady Day and (John Coltrane)', parallel 7th chords, bar 65)
- Change of harmonic rhythm, i.e. rate of chord changes per bar (final section of 'Lady Day and (John Coltrane)', from bar 119)
- Use of basic (non-extended) chords (opening of 'Love and Affection')
- Primary chords ('Love and Affection', bar 22 onwards)
- Chromatic side-stepping ('Love and Affection', bar 62 onwards).

Tonality and structure

- 'Inner State (of Mind)' is in C minor with a modal (two flat) key signature. Its structure is freely evolving, with the recurring 'Inner State' motif, instrumentals and alternating verse (supported by riff) and rap sections
- 'Lady Day and (John Coltrane)' is also in C minor. It is a modified 12-bar blues with introduction and extended coda
- 'Love and Affection' opens in C♯ minor but continues in E major. Its freely evolving structure starts with an introduction before moving into a riff-based song with a prominent refrain.

'Cloudbusting', 'And Dream of Sheep' and 'Under Ice' from *Hounds of Love* (Kate Bush)

Context

- Kate Bush (b.1958) is a performer and composer of progressive rock
- Her music sometimes contains Irish elements, stemming from her family connections
- The album *Hounds of Love* was released in 1985 and draws on vocals, piano (played by Bush), balalaika, string sextet, bouzouki and uilleann pipes
- The album was produced by Bush in her own studio
- In part, it could be classed as a concept album: the first side of the original vinyl recording consists of five progressive rock songs; the second side, 'The Ninth Wave', was based very loosely on Tennyson's poetic work *Idylls of the King*
- 'Cloudbusting' is the last of the progressive rock songs on side one of the vinyl. It is based on incidents in the life and career of the psychologist Wilhelm Reich
- The first two songs from the original side two, 'And Dream of Sheep' and 'Under Ice', depict the thoughts of a drowning girl.

'Cloudbusting' is based on Bush's reading of Peter Reich's *A Book of Dreams*, and in particular the imprisonment and death of psychoanalyst Wilhelm Reich (1897–1957) in the USA.

Notation

In the Anthology, staff notation is used with guitar chords indicated above the system. Speeds are indicated in beats per minute, but variations in tempo and dynamic signs are given in a traditional form. Each song uses a different type of layout, as follows:

- 'Cloudbusting' is a full score. The string sextet parts are mainly printed on two staves, but occasionally the more active violin parts are allotted a separate stave. Parts for voice, backing vocals, three keyboards, balalaika and percussion are scored separately
- 'And Dream of Sheep' is notated for voice and piano, with additional staves introduced as required for bouzouki and whistles
- 'Under Ice' is a short score, with parts indicated as required on three or four staves.

Sonority

A wide range of resources and timbres are employed in the three prescribed works:

- Though vocals, Fairlight CMI (Computer Musical Instrument, i.e. synthesiser) and drums play a major role in 'Cloudbusting', the most distinctive timbre is the string sextet (calling to mind 'Eleanor Rigby' by The Beatles). There are also occasional appearances of balalaika
- 'And Dream of Sheep' is the most conventional popular music timbre of the three songs, with voice and piano dominating. There are also additional parts for bouzouki (a plucked string instrument used in Greek and modern Irish music) and whistles. The sound is further intensified by the use of dubbed voices
- Unusual atmospheric timbres are created in 'Under Ice' through the use of synthesised strings and a low vocal tessitura.

Textures

Melody-dominated homophony predominates throughout, but notice particularly:

- Persistent detached chords for strings in 'Cloudbusting', as well as:
  - Fragmentary patterns on keyboard
  - Counter-melody in octaves in the violin
  - Expansion of texture with the three lowest strings and keyboard 3 providing sustained semibreves
- Broken-chord figures in 'And Dream of Sheep'
- The lean sound in 'Under Ice' is created by the fragmentary vocal line, supported by bass octaves and two-part synthesised string motifs, mainly in 4ths and 5ths; a soft synth pad sounds throughout.

Tempo, metre and rhythm

'Cloudbusting'

This song is in a moderate, rather mechanical strict time. The time signature is mainly quadruple, with occasional changes (to $\frac{6}{4}$ and $\frac{2}{4}$).

Rhythmic features include:

- Constant crotchet beat established at the start by the strings
- Steady, reinforcing crotchet drum-beats from bar 11
- Backbeat
- Mechanical patterns in the violin (see bar 3)

- Effective halt to the mechanical rhythms at key words, e.g. 'I won't forget' (bar 50)
- Semibreves in the lower parts (bar 95), combined with a strong rhythmic figure in the upper string parts.
- Longer note values in the violin counter-melody beginning in bar 34, and in the additional synthesised line at bar 65
- Syncopation, e.g. keyboard 2 (bar 69–70).

'Dream of Sheep'

This song uses a moderately slow quadruple metre with occasional changes of signature. Rubato, rits and fermata ⌢ are employed. Notice the use of dotted rhythm, triplets and Scotch snap.

'Under Ice'

In this song, the tempo speeds up from 65 beats per minute to 108 and then slows at the close. The metre is largely irregular, starting and ending in quadruple time but frequently alternating with triple time sections.

Other prominent rhythmic features include:

- A two quaver–crotchet pattern, first heard in strings and taken over in the voice part
- A two-note figure with longer second note (vocal part, bars 12–13, 'so white')
- The long-sustained synth pad, which enters in bar 2
- Scotch snaps (e.g. bar 27)
- Triplets (e.g. bar 50).

Melody

'Cloudbusting'

- Modal, based in C♯ Aeolian minor with occasional focus on B major
- Lead vocal is a minor 10th, from G♯ below middle C to B above
- Word setting is predominantly syllabic, with very occasional slurred pairs
- Opens with leaps of 3rds, 4ths and 5ths, but then narrows in range
- Portamento
- Other melodic features include:
  - The violin's opening narrow-range motif, featuring some chromaticism
  - The violin's later counter-melody, with step-wise descent
  - An additional melody line in keyboard 2, starting at bar 65
  - Bvox vocalisation with leap of minor 7th (bar 111).

'And Dream of Sheep'

- E major
- Vocal range is a major 9th (B–C♯), though for the most part occupies the lower part of this span (B–G♯)
- Distinctive perfect 5ths in the opening phrase
- Repeated notes
- Word setting is mainly syllabic, with brief melismas at phrase-endings
- Repeated 3rds at 'If they find me racing…'.

'Under Ice'

- Vocal range is a minor 10th (A–C), with low notes favoured for the most part
- Characterised by a mainly step-wise two-pitch figure
- A more lyrical phrase occurs at 'The river has frozen over', with leaps of 4ths and a 5th
- Word-setting is mainly syllabic, with some slurred pairs
- Descending chromatic portamento at close.

Harmony

'Cloudbusting'

- The song's mechanical feel is intensified through the frequent use of a limited number of dissonant added-note chords (C♯m⁷ – B major with added 9th – A major with added 9th and 6th, and the occasional G♯ minor chord with added 4th)
- All chords contain both B and C♯
- Harmonic rhythm is varied: e.g. at the opening the C♯ and B chords have two beats; whereas at bar 95, the chords are allotted four beats.

'And Dream of Sheep'

- Functional harmony in the key of E major
- Typical chords include I, IIb, V, VI⁷, IV with added 9th
- Tonic pedal at 'If they find me racing…'
- A chord of perfect 4ths played on whistles at bar 41.

'Under Ice'

- Conventional chords avoided
- Bass hints at functional structure, with the tonic (A), submediant (F), mediant (C), and subdominant (D)
- The dominant (E) is avoided.

Tonality and structure

'Cloudbusting'

This song is in C♯ minor with no modulation. Broadly, the song follows a verse and chorus pattern with instrumentals:

Bars	Section
1-8	Verse
9-18	Bridge
18-33	Chorus
34-41	Verse
42-51	Bridge
51-68	Chorus
69-81	Instrumental, involving synthesised melody
81-98	Chorus
99-136	Instrumental and coda, featuring chorus material and Bvox

'And Dream of Sheep'

This song is in E major throughout, and is loosely strophic:

Bars	Section
1-15	Verse
15-19	Link 1
19-36	Verse
36-40	Link 2
40-53	Coda

'Under Ice'

The bass notes indicate clearly that this song is in A minor. The tonality is clouded at the end by the chromaticism and background electronic effects.

The song is through-composed, with alternating fragmentary melodic motifs:

Bars	Section
1–8	Introduction
8–13	Motif 1
14–18	Motif 2
19–24	Motif 1
24–29	Motif 2
30–39	Motif 1
40–45	Motif 2
46–58	Motif 1 and coda

AREA OF STUDY 5:

Fusions

Estampes: No. 1: 'Pagodes' and No. 2: 'La Soirée dans Grenade' (Debussy)

Context

- *Estampes* (*'Prints'*) was written in 1903
- It was the first of Debussy's piano works to be regarded as truly impressionistic – a term first applied to the work of such painters as Monet
- Notice in this respect:
  - Emphasis on colour and texture
  - Use of the piano's sustain pedal to blend sonorities
  - Music that was not designed to be programmatic so much as allusive
- There are three pieces in *Estampes*, the last of which (not prescribed here) is 'Jardins sous la pluie' ('Gardens in the rain'), based on a French folk song
- The prescribed works show influences of Indonesian gamelan music ('Pagodes') and Spanish music ('La soirée dans Grenade')
- Debussy first became acquainted with the Javanese gamelan at the Paris World Exhibition in 1889, and it clearly influenced the sonority and melodic content of 'Pagodes' (use of pentatonic scale).

> Regarding programmatic music, Debussy once remarked that music should not be 'confined to reproducing, more or less exactly, Nature, but the mysterious correspondences which link Nature with Imagination'. In reality, this approach is more symbolist than impressionist, as the work of art becomes a symbol of a concept or idea, rather than a specific evocation of the real world.

Notation

- 'Pagodes' is notated throughout on the two staves typically used in piano music
- 'La Soirée dans Grenade' resorts to three staves at bars 96–109 and bars 130–end

- Conventional dynamic marks are employed
- Many other performance directions are in French, though Debussy uses some Italian (e.g. *rubato*, *tempo giusto*)
- Vague pedal directions are given in 'Pagodes' and are only specifically printed for the last seven bars of 'La soirée dans Grenade'. However, from the style of writing, it is clear that the sustaining pedal is essential throughout. '2 Ped' indicates sustain pedal and una corda ('soft pedal') together.

Sonority

- Both pieces use very nearly the full range of the piano:
  - In 'Pagodes' from lowest B to highest A♯
  - In 'La soirée dans Grenade' from lowest C♯ to top C♯
- Washes of sound are created in 'Pagodes' through use of sustaining pedal
- A more brittle staccato articulation is used on occasion in 'La Soirée dans Grenade'
- Una corda pedal contributes to the characteristic timbre of 'Pagodes'.

Una corda is the left-foot pedal on the piano, which aids the creation of a softer, almost muffled sound.

Textures

'Pagodes'

The textures vary considerably in density and type, with dynamics ranging from delicate at the start to massive fortissimo at the climax:

- Layered homophony (bars 1–2)
- Melody-dominated homophony (bar 3) with double pedal (drone)
- Melody-dominated homophony with additional inner part (bar 7)
- Two-part counterpoint (bar 11)
- Brief imitation (bar 23)
- Left-hand chords with a high, bell-like right hand
- Rapid ornamental right-hand figuration, melody in middle range, long bass notes (bar 78).

'La Soirée dans Grenade'

The texture draws on various types of homophony, often layered; dynamics range from ***ppp*** to ***ff***.

Notice particularly the following features:

- Monophonic – melody in left hand with inverted pedal in right hand (bar 7)
- Chords with single sustained bass note (bar 17)
- Homophonic; melody in octaves (bar 38)
- Three layers – melody transferred to middle part, chords above, habanera rhythm in bass (bar 51).

Tempo, metre and rhythm

'Pagodes'

- The tempo is 'modérément animé' (moderately quickly), with frequent use of ritardando
- The time signature is simple quadruple ($\frac{4}{4}$), with two bars of $\frac{2}{4}$ (bars 92 and 94)
- Notice the following features:
  - Syncopation (e.g. bar 1)
  - Tied notes over bar lines, undermining a strong sense of first-beat accent (e.g. bars 3–4)
  - Triplets (e.g. bar 11)
  - Quintuplets (e.g. bar 80)
  - Hetero-rhythms, or cross-rhythms, typically twos against threes (e.g. bar 23), eight demi-semiquavers against three quavers (e.g. bar 78)
  - Long gong-like sounds in bass.

'La Soirée dans Grenade'

A distinguishing feature in this piece is its habanera rhythm:

- Debussy indicates that the tempo is 'movement de Habanera', and that the piece should begin slowly in a nonchalantly graceful rhythm ('Commencer lentement dans un rhythme nonchalamment gracieux')
- It is in duple time ($\frac{2}{4}$), with sudden switches to triple time ($\frac{3}{4}$) at bars 109 and 115

- There are also indications that the performer should alternate between *rubato* and *tempo giusto* (strict time)
- Note also the following rhythmic features:
  - Triplets (e.g. bars 9 and 15)
  - Syncopation (e.g. bars 11, 33–36, 67)
  - Hetero-rhythm (twos against threes) (e.g. bar 34)
  - Scotch snaps (e.g. bars 35 and 36).

Melody

'Pagodes'

Much of the melody is built on:

- Two-bar phrases
- Pentatonic structures
- Its first melodic line consists of just four pitches: G♯–C♯–D♯–F♯; the fifth note of this pentatonic scale (B) is supplied in the accompanying harmonic structure:

Pagodes, bar 3 (melody and bass only)

This melody is rhythmically varied through the introduction of triplets at bar 11.

- A change of pentatonic pattern in the melody at bars 15–18 to G♯–A♯–C♯–D♯–F
- A whole-tone element occurs in the melody of the central section (bar 33): see the line E♯–D♯–C♯–B
- A final pentatonic motif can be heard at bar 37, drawing on the original set of pitches.

'La Soirée dans Grenade'

This piece is built on a limited number of melodic motifs:

- The orientalist 'Andalusian'-Arabic melody at bar 7. Note particularly the lining up of semitone and augmented 2nd (bracketed in the example over the page).

La Soirée dans Grenade, bars 7-16 (melody only)

- Other features of the melody above include:
  - Acciaccaturas
  - A limited range (an octave, with much of the melody in the upper half)
  - Avoidance of balanced phrasing
- Theme 2 at bar 17 featuring:
  - Balanced two-bar phrases
  - Repeated notes
- Theme 3 at bar 23, featuring whole-tone elements
- Extension of theme 2 with a loose descending sequence built on descending 3rds (bars 33–36)
- Theme 4 (bar 41) in major mode with lengthy descent:

La Soirée dans Grenade, bars 41-50 (melody)

Harmony

'Pagodes'

The harmony in this piece is strongly affected by the pentatonic content of the melody.

Significant aspects include:

- Its static quality
- Slow harmonic rhythm

- 'Changing background' approach, i.e. changing harmonisations of the same melody
- The added 6th (B–D#–F#–G#) at the start

Other prominent landmarks include:

- Extended chords, e.g. B^{13} (bar 7)
- Diminished triad (bar 16^2)
- Colouristic, isolated major 2nd (bar 32)
- Pentatonic harmonisation at bar 37, with parallelism and open 5th chords.

'La Soirée dans Grenade'

The harmonic vocabulary is much more varied in this piece than in 'Pagodes'.

Typical devices include:

- Pedal points
- Parallel 7th chords (e.g. bar 17)
- Whole-tone harmonies (e.g. bar 23)
- False relations between adjacent chords (e.g. bar 33)
- Open 5ths chords (e.g. bar 38)
- Chords of 5ths and 4ths (bar 38, last quaver)
- Simultaneous false relation (e.g. bar 52)
- Parallel triads (bars 109–110).

Structure and tonality

'Pagodes'

- Ternary form with coda
- Static harmonies mean that it remains close to B major, though the central section (bars 33–53) moves into the region of F# major/D# minor.

'La Soirée dans Grenade'

- A succession of different themes, with some repetition
- The opening 'Arabic' theme returns at the end and closes in the tonic major
- The major mode theme (beginning bar 38) is repeated once (beginning bar 97)
- Most keys are related to the tonic of F# minor
- Keys are reinforced through the use of pedal points
- Tonality is weakened, however, by the use of whole-tone harmony
- The two interruptions in triple time also contrast dramatically, by being in the keys of C mixolydian (bar 109) and A mixolydian (bar 115).

'Allá va candela' and 'Se quema la chumbambá' from *Caña Quema*: (La Familia Valera Miranda)

Context

- The two prescribed excerpts are examples of Cuban music from the Oriente region in the east of the country, which has Santiago de Cuba as its main city
- The fusion of styles here involves a blending of an essentially European (Spanish) element with Latin American features, some of which also had links with African music
- The Spanish element is evident in the use of guitars, cuatro and double bass, and the use of a functional harmonic language
- The Afro-Cuban influence is evident in the use of maracas, bongos and claves
- The two songs date back to the early part of the 20th century and were the work of earlier generations of La Familia Valera Miranda, the performers of the excerpts.

> La Familia Valera Miranda (the Valera Miranda family) in the 19th century worked on the land, producing sugar cane and trees for timber; several members of the family were involved in the struggle against Spanish colonialists, culminating in the establishing of the independent Republic of Cuba in 1902.

- Cuban music is often intended for dancing and usually originated in improvisation
- Subject matter could be political, or humorous retellings of incidents in the life of the family:
    - 'Se quema la chumbambá' ('Our land is burning') is concerned with the family matriarch's dismissive reaction to news that a fire had broken out on the Valera's farm
    - 'Allá va candela' ('There goes Mr Fire') mocks one of the members of the band who had fallen madly in love
- The band consists of vocalists, guitar, cuatro, double bass and percussion instruments (bongos, maracas, claves).

Notation

- Both songs are initially notated in full score in the Anthology
- Once basic patterns are established in the accompanying section, large parts of each song are given in reduced form – i.e. only the vocal part is given in 'Se quema la chumbambá' and vocal part with cuatro in 'Allá va candela'
- Significant changes in the other instruments are notated when they arise, and the conclusions of both songs are given in full score
- The cuatro solos in both songs are notated in full
- Tempo indications are in beats per minute
- There are a limited number of traditional dynamic marks and accent signs.

Dance types

Cuban music included such types of dance as habanera (see Debussy's 'La Soirée dans Grenade'), canción, son and bolero. 'Se quema la chumbambá' is a son (regarded as a forerunner of the salsa), while 'Allá va candela' opens as a bolero before morphing into a son.

Son characteristics:

- Use of call and response
- Duple metre
- 3-2 son clave pattern forming a two-bar pattern with three notes in the first and two in the second:

- A limited harmonic scheme, typically of tonic and dominant chords
- Vocal part based on Spanish metrical patterns
- Strophic structure, perhaps with instrumental part-way through.

Bolero characteristics:

- Associated with romantic subjects
- Moderate duple time (as distinct from the European bolero in triple time)
- The bolero tends to be more lyrical than the son.

Sonority

- Performing forces in both numbers are:
  - Solo male voice (Pregón) and male-voice chorus (Coro)
  - Cuatro (a guitar-like instrument with four 'courses' (sets) of two strings)
  - Guitar

- Plucked double bass
- Maracas, claves and bongo.

Texture

- Melody-dominated homophony predominates in both songs
- The coro in 'Se quema' is homophonic (homorhythmic), with the two parts singing in 3rds, 6ths, diminished 5ths and perfect 4ths
- In 'Allá va candela', the coro is confined to interjections of two notes in octaves
- Monophony (cuatro) can be heard at the opening of both songs
- The cuatro solos in both songs involve some multi-stopping.

Tempo, metre and rhythm

'Se quema la chumbambá'

- Brisk duple time
- 3-2 son claves (see example above in 'son characteristics')
- Constant quavers on bongo
- Syncopation (e.g. cuatro solo, bar 83)
- A three-crotchet rhythm every fourth bar of vocals
- Triplets in passing in cuatro solo.

'Allá va candela'

- Moderate duple time, typical of bolero-son at start
- An accelerando at bar 39 leads into the brisker son
- Flowing quavers on cuatro at start
- Anacrusis in vocal part
- Dotted rhythms
- Syncopations (cuatro, bar 5).

Melody

Both numbers are characterised by balanced phrasing.

'Se quema la chumbambá'

- Vocal lines draw on first six notes of G minor scale
- The lead vocal's line begins on the dominant
- Cuatro introduction uses broken chord patterns
- Chromatic elements and bigger leaps appear in cuatro solo.

'Allá va candela'

- Vocal lines draw on all notes within the scale of E major
- Solo vocal line spans a 12th (B–F♯)
- Falling 5ths at ends of phrases
- Rapidly repeated notes represent a feverishly beating heart
- Cuatro's solo is marked by chromaticism (bars 75–76) and ornamentation (acciaccaturas and slides).

Harmony

A limited range of chords is used in both songs.

'Se quema la chumbambá'

- Tonic and dominant 7th chords
- Additional E♭ on cuatro creates a brief dominant 9th and outlines of diminished 7th chords
- C major is touched on in the cuatro solo at bars 89–90.

'Allá va candela'

- Tonic (with occasional added 6th) in cuatro and dominant 7th (plus 9th)
- Harmony expanded with reference to subdominant (e.g. bar 29)
- Cuatro ranges more widely with parallel 4ths (bar 75) and V^{11} (bar 79)

Structure and tonality

'Se quema la chumbambá'

- G minor without modulation
- Alternating verse and refrain, broken at one point by an extended cuatro solo.

'Allá va candela'

- E major without modulation
- The structure is less regular than that of 'Se quema', as follows:
  - Introduction and bolero material ('Tengo la boca' and 'Corazón'), which is not subsequently repeated
  - 'Desde los pies' (bars 32–38)
  - Allá va candela chorus – solo vocal and coro (repeated)
  - Extended cuatro solo
  - Truncated reference to chorus (bars 124–138) followed by repeat of 'Desde los pies'
  - Repeat of 'Allá va candela' chorus (solo vocal and coro) with solo vocal improvisation.

AREA OF STUDY 6:
New directions

Three Dances for Two Prepared Pianos: No. 1 (John Cage)

Context

- John Cage (1912–1992) was an American avant-garde composer
- He was a pupil of Henry Cowell (1897–1965), who experimented with extreme chromaticism, rhythmic complexity, graphic notation and extended piano techniques
- Some of Cage's most notable works stemmed from his work as an accompanist for the dancer and choreographer, Merce Cunningham
- An interest in providing percussion music for dance led Cage to develop the 'prepared piano' in an attempt to economise on both space and expense
- A prepared piano involved alteration of the piano's timbres through insertion of various items between the strings
- His most famous prepared piano work is *Sonatas and Interludes* (1948)
- The prescribed work – for two amplified prepared pianos – was completed in 1945 and was eventually used for dance purposes by Cunningham in *Dromenon* (1947)
- Cage's works reflect interests in:
  - Eastern philosophy and religion (*Sonatas and Interludes*)
  - The role of silence (*4'33"*)
  - Aleatoric music, or 'chance music' (*Music of Changes*).

Notation

- Full score with traditional staff notation
- Notice, however, that accidentals apply only to the note they precede and not to the whole bar
- Boxed numerals above the score act as reference points, indicating the start of a new phrase in the underlying structure
- Tempo is indicated by beats per minute
- Conventional dynamic indications are used

SET WORKS 65

AREA OF STUDY 6: NEW DIRECTIONS

- In the Anthology, pedals are indicated with the directions 'una corda' ('quiet pedal'), 'tre corde' (end quiet pedal) and the standard 'Ped' sign to refer to the sustaining pedal.
- The score is preceded by instructions for preparing the instrument for performance.

Sonority

- Sonority and timbre depend on the preparations that Cage prescribed
- Preparation involves the insertion of so-called 'mutes' between the strings of the piano keys used
- Different materials are employed, e.g. metal bolts and screws, weather strip, rubber, plastic, coins
- Only the prepared notes appear in the course of the composition, and not all keys of the pianos have to be prepared
- A range of timbres results, from dead to gong-like
- Pitch, however, is distorted considerably, meaning that the score cannot be taken as a reliable guide to the resulting sound
- Though preparation instructions are detailed, it would be impossible to create the exact same effect from one performance to another.

Dynamics

- The dynamic level is mainly soft
- For extended sections there is little dynamic change (e.g. the opening part)
- There is an effective contrast between *ppp* just before phrase 36 and *ff* at phrase 38
- Accents are frequently employed (e.g. right hand of piano 1, phrases 38–40).

Texture

- The texture is mainly contrapuntal, with the two piano parts frequently working independently
- A two-part texture is used for each piano
- Other features to note include:
  - Monophony (phrase 5, from bar 14)
  - A sort of melody-dominated homophony (from phrase 38)
  - Homorhythm (from phrase 7).

Tempo, metre and rhythm

- Tempo is a fast duple time ($\frac{2}{2}$) throughout, at 88 minims per minute (not 88 crotchets per minute, as is written in the Anthology score)
- Note values are largely quavers and crotchets

- Duple metre is disrupted through cross-rhythms, mainly groupings of three quavers at a time (see piano 1 opening)
- Piano 2 works against piano 1's opening rhythm with a steady crotchet pattern in the left hand and off-beat quavers in the right hand
- Notice, however, that the left hand figure in piano 2 consists of a seven crotchet ostinato, also working against the written duple time.

Structure

- Like many works of this period, Cage's structure for this piece is based on a fractal mathematical approach, also known as micro-macrocosmic design
- Here the proportions used on a small scale also operate on the movement's overall structure:
  - Dance No. 1 consists of nine 30-bar parts
  - Each part is sub-divided into nine phrases, signalled by the boxed numerals in the score
  - The phrases in all parts have the following bar-lengths: 2 5 2 – 2 6 2 – 2 7 2
  - It is highly unlikely that the listener is aware of these proportions in performance, but notice how the length of the central subdivision progressively increases by a bar a time (i.e. from 5 to 6 to 7)
- Thus, traditional large-scale dance forms are avoided, but there are some repetitions, e.g. the final 30-bar section is a repeat of the one preceding
- There are a number of other smaller-scale repetitions, including the reappearance of a number of motifs from the first two parts in the final parts, e.g. the three-quaver motif from phrase 5 returns at phrases 64 and 73.

Tonality

There can be no sense of tonality underpinning the movement's structure, given the nature of a prepared piano. In other words, there are no exact pitches creating a hierarchy of sounds revolving around a tonic.

Melody and harmony

For the same reason (indeterminate, unfixed pitch), it is impossible to speak of melodic line or harmonic content. In other words, rhythm and sonority prevail throughout.

FURTHER LISTENING

Try comparing Cage's approach to rhythm with Messiaen's use of iso-rhythms in e.g. *Quatuor pour le fin du temps*.

Petals [for Cello Solo and Optional Electronics] (Kaija Saariaho)

Context

- Kaija Saariaho is a leading Finnish composer, born in Helsinki in 1952
- She has produced a significant body of work in which electronics play an important role, e.g. the recent theatre piece *Only the Sound Remains* (2015)
- In *Petals*, the cello is combined with ongoing live electronics, as opposed to pre-recorded electronic sounds
- *Petals* was written for Anssi Karttunen, who first performed the work at a festival of contemporary music in Bremen in 1988
- The title of the work refers to the petal of the waterlily, and is an off-shoot of *Nymph*éa [*Waterlily*], dating from 1987, scored for string quartet and electronics
- According to the composer, *Petals* is concerned with the opposition of 'fragile colouristic passages' to 'more energetic events with clear rhythmic and melodic character', which in turn are subjected to a number of transformations.

Notation

- The basis of the score is conventional staff notation
- There are, however, no bars or bar numbers. Instead, each of the 30 lines in the piece is numbered, and we will refer to these lines as 'staves'
- Indications for use of reverb and harmoniser (see below) are placed under each stave
- At some points, the notation is indeterminate, i.e. aleatoric with regard to melodic and rhythmic elements
- Notation is expanded by the addition of various symbols indicating specific effects not covered by traditional notation, as follows:
  - Horizontal arrow – a gradual change from one sound or way of playing to another
  - Diminuendo hairpin closing with a small zero – reduction in volume to absolute silence
  - Crescendo hairpin starting with small zero – increase in volume, commencing from silence
  - Arrow-head pointing upwards – highest note possible
  - Filled in black crescendo sign – add bow pressure to produce a scratching sound, i.e. pitch is replaced by noise (and vice versa for diminuendo sign)

- See the introductory comments in the Anthology score for other symbols, notably those for quarter-tones and various types of glissando.

Sonority

- The work blends traditional cello timbres with extended techniques and various degrees of electronic distortion

Acoustic

- Traditional cello playing (bowed, pitched sound) can be heard in the music of staves 10–13
- Articulation includes slurs (e.g. stave 5) and staccato (e.g. stave 4)
- Extended techniques include:
  - Lengthy trills and tremolos for colouristic effect
  - Harmonics (usually artificial), often combined with ordinary notes (see stave 14) and more strikingly with another harmonic (stave 15)
  - Glissandos (with varying degrees of vibrato and/or with harmonics)
  - Micro-intervals
  - Scratchy tone (noise) produced by use of more bow pressure than usual.

Electronic

- Live electronics most importantly involve:
  - Digital reverb with variable reverb
  - Harmoniser
- Reverb time is set at 2.5 seconds, increasing to 15 seconds in stave 21 and finally 30 seconds at the close
- The introductory remarks in the Anthology state that the reverb should result in a 'clear and bright sound' and that if there is any doubt as to how much to apply, 'too little rather than too much' is preferable
- In any event, the degree of reverb varies between 20% and 50%
- The harmoniser shifts pitches by a quarter-tone and then combines this transposed sound with the original, typically during scratchy bowing sections to maximise colouristic distortion effects. (See introductory remarks for details on preferred models of harmoniser.)

Dynamics

The range is extreme: from sounds pulled out of silence, through *pppp* to *ffff*. Saariaho requires a 'clear and rich, close sound', stipulating that microphones should be placed as close as possible to the instrument and that the general level be set rather loud, but 'not painfully so'.

Texture

- In the more conventionally played passages, the cello line could be described as monophonic (e.g. stave 10)
- Double stopping occurs in stave 11 and is used to create harmonics in staves 14–16
- Effective use is made of two-part writing in stave 17, where the lowest string on the instrument (open C) is left ringing while material is played on higher strings
- Colouristic block-sounds result in the scratchy bowing passages with harmoniser, but these are far removed from the homophony of traditional textures. In fact, it is probably more useful to approach the topic of texture in terms of relative densities of sound.

Tempo, metre and rhythm

- **Tempo** moves between lento sections and faster moving passages
- *Lento* passages, as at the start, should move so slowly that staves in these sections should always last at least 20 seconds. The final section of the work is extremely slow, with the last stave taking at least 55 seconds to perform
- There is no **metre** discernable in terms of time signatures and bars
- Written note-lengths in the *lento* sections employ semibreves but are to be regarded as pulseless sounds of indeterminate length
- The passage beginning at stave 10 seems to be more precisely notated regarding **rhythms**, but pulse cannot be detected because of the irregularity of groupings, ornaments, ties, glissando and fermata (pauses).

Melody

- Melodic content is typically found in the faster moving sections (lento passages tend to be colouristic rather than melodic)
- In the energico section beginning at stave 4, a scurrying line can be heard, made up of quarter tones (microtones) and glissandos
- The second such section, at stave 10, is more conventionally melodic with clearly defined intervallic content, often of an angular nature (notice the intervals of a major 7th (stave 10) and augmented 4th (stave 12)
- Some other characteristics of this section include:
  - Repeated note figuration (stave 11)
  - Short descending figures (beginning on stave 11). The starting note of each descent rises, with the high-point occuring in stave 13
  - Ornamentation

- The poco impetuoso at stave 17 is characterised by agitated figures, initially semitonal
- From stave 23, striking use of glissandos rising alternately to C♯ and F♯ are supported by 'pedal' low (open string) Cs
- The section culminates with a glissando to the highest pitch available (stave 27).

Harmony

- There is no sense of harmonic progression, though there are very brief moments when distinguishable pitches are heard, e.g. stave 15
- It could be said that one traditional harmonic device is the lengthy pedal C at staves 15–28
- Notice the prominent high F♯s which appear at stave 23, seemingly forming a tritonal dominant with the pedal C.

Tritonal dominants can be found in Herrmann's music for the film *Psycho*. Briefly they arise from the replacing of the traditional dominant with one an augmented 4th or diminished 5th above the tonic.

Tonality

- Tonality (in terms of a hierarchy of pitches) is scarcely relevant in *Petals*, partly because of the absence of functional harmonic progressions
- However, the persistent use of the pedal C from stave 15 could be regarded as a tonal anchor, even though the work is primarily colouristic.

Structure

- *Petals* is one continuous movement
- There are elements of short-term repetition of motifs. For example, the treatment of the glissando figures from stave 23

■ The work depends on the alternation of what the composer describes as 'fragile colouristic passages' with 'more energetic events with clear rhythmic and melodic character':

Tempo	Staves
Lento	1–3
'energico'	4–7
Lento	8–9
'espressivo'	10–13
Lento	13–16
'poco impetuoso'	17–27
'dolcissimo' (This marking appears as 'Lento' in the original Hansen edition)	27–30

FURTHER LISTENING

It would be useful to investigate works by other Finnish composers:

■ Sibelius, Symphonies Nos 4 and 5, and the tone poem *Tapiola*

■ Rautavaara, *Cantus Arcticus* (scored for orchestra with pre-recorded birdsong)

For a fine example of another contemporary composer's approach to cello technique, listen to Lutosławski's Cello Concerto.

Sample materials for Question 6 (Section B, essay 2)

This chapter provides examples of the types of question normally set for Section B, essay 2. You may find it helpful to bear in mind the following points:

1. The Specification and Edexcel's Sample Assessment Materials (SAMs) state two assessment objectives:

   - The demonstration and application of musical knowledge (Assessment Objective 3 **[AO3]**)

   - The use of analytical and appraising skills leading to evaluation and critical judgement about the work in question (Assessment Objective 4 **[AO4]**).

   The other assessment objectives concern performance issues (AO1) and composition skills (AO2).

2. You will have a good idea what to expect before going into the exam room, as the essay questions are distinctly formulaic. All the essays in the SAMs open with the command word 'evaluate', before going on to name the aspects of the work on which you should focus (typically two out of structure, tonality, metre, rhythm, melody, harmony, texture, sonority etc.). You are also requested to relate your discussion to other relevant works.

3. The command words relevant to this type of question are:

   - **Evaluate** – make judgements about the stipulated elements and go on to draw conclusions

   - **Analyse** – investigate and pick out musical features and show how these features contribute to the effect created

   - **Discuss** – this may involve setting out the issues raised by the question; considering the various aspects arising in the course of the investigation; and applying a reasoned approach in the presentation of the response.

4. In fact, all these aspects will be closely interlinked as analytical comment will provide evidence for your appraisal.

5. At AS level, the marks for this question are evenly split between AO3 and AO4, with ten marks going to each assessment objective.

6. The final mark is awarded on the basis of a 'general impression', rather than the awarding of marks for individual comments. The mark schemes that follow show how this system could operate in practice. As a first step, compare the following statements concerning the Piano Trio by Clara Schumann:

'A dominant pedal occurs at bars 155–164.'

'The dominant pedal occurring at bars 155–164 creates a sense of anticipation, preparing for the start of the recapitulation.'

The first statement is accurate and would be credited under AO3. The second statement is not only worthy of credit under AO3, but in assessing its effect within the overall structure it also qualifies for credit under AO4.

See the grid provided in the SAM Mark Scheme for details of the four levels that examiners will consider in scoring the final mark. The lowest level (Marks 1–5) refers to 'limited awareness of contextual factors' and 'limited identification of musical elements', 'little reference to texts', 'limited organisation of ideas' and 'little attempt to link to other relevant works'. In contrast, the top level (Marks 16–20) expects that the candidate will make 'detailed links between the music and ... context', will accurately identify a wide range of musical elements, construct a 'controlled argument' and make good use of terminology with reference to 'relevant works ... to justify points'.

7. Your answers in this section should be in continuous prose. If you write in note form or use bullet points, you will not be awarded marks in the highest band. On the other hand, if you are running out of time, it would still be sensible to offer information in note form, providing that your notes are clear.

8. Finally, remember that you will be provided with a resources booklet, which contains representative extracts from the works in question. You will not have access to the complete Anthology, so you must develop a good overall grasp of the prescribed works by way of preparation and be able to find ways of locating devices and various sections without necessarily using bar numbers.

Read the following questions carefully so that you are sure about the sort of information you are required to produce. If you are uncertain about what is meant, refer to the terminology section earlier in the book.

Vocal music

Evaluate the use of sonority and texture in Movement 1 of J. S. Bach's Cantata 'Ein feste Burg'.

Relate your discussion to other relevant works. These may include set works, wider listening or other music.

Mark scheme

Before studying the mark scheme (indicative content) below, attempt the question yourself. You will find it useful to compare your answer with the mark scheme and the sample answer that follows.

The expression 'indicative content' used by examination boards simply refers to the sort of information that examiners look for when marking students' exam papers.

Indicative content

Answers should show in equal proportions an ability to apply musical knowledge (AO3 ('Assessment Objective 3')) and to offer evaluations and critical judgements about the music **[AO4]**:

Performing forces

- The cantata is a late-Baroque work for use in a Lutheran church service, in which the Lutheran chorale plays a major part **[AO4]**
- As might be expected, sonorities are characteristic of the era. Movement 1 is scored for:
    - (Small) four-part chorus (SATB)
    - Three oboes including a taille (an early cor anglais)

- Strings consisting of violins I and II, viola, cello and violone (used in the Baroque era in place of double bass)
  - Continuo instruments (organ and cembalo [harpsichord]) **[AO3]**
- Violins and viola double SAT, but cello shadows the bass, sometimes elaborating in heterophony. **[AO3]**

Texture

- Movement 1 is contrapuntal:
  - Imitative writing in the vocal parts in fugal style
  - The subject in tenor is an ornate version of the chorale melody
  - The subject lasts five bars (a rather unusual length)
  - The answer appears in alto
  - The counter-subject is based on the second phrase of the chorale
  - Canon at the octave, directly quoting the chorale 'Ein feste Burg', is heard in oboes and violone, with a half-bar between entries **[AO3]**
- The texture is further complicated by the heterophony in the cello at bars 20–22 **[AO3]**
- Bach very often adopted a similar approach in his choruses, with a fugal texture for most voices, and the chorale highlighted in another part, e.g. the cantata 'Wachet auf' **[AO4]**
- Canon was often used in Bach's writing to convey strongly an important idea, e.g. the canon in the Creed of the B minor Mass **[AO4]**
- Fugue was also used by other Baroque composers, e.g. Handel's *Messiah* 'And with his stripes', but the simultaneous use of canon heard in the Bach cantata is unusual. **[AO4]**

Sample answer

Mark this answer yourself, commenting on its good points and whether these satisfy AO3, AO4 or both. In addition, make a note of any aspects which could have been improved. Check your assessment against the examiner's comments that follow, after completing your marking.

Bach's Cantata No. 80, 'Ein feste Burg', is an eight-movement work, probably written in 1730 specially to celebrate the Festival of the Lutheran Reformation. As this was an important day in the Lutheran calendar, the work is relatively richly scored with soprano, tenor and bass soloists, a four-part chorus (soprano, alto, tenor and bass), three oboes and a string group. Another, even more grand version also included parts for trumpets and timpani.

adding to the ceremonial nature of the piece, but this version was not by Bach himself, but probably by W. F Bach, one of his sons.

These performing forces are typical of the late Baroque era, and the resulting sonorities are peculiar to this period. The third oboe was in actual fact a 'taille', the predecessor of the modern cor anglais, and in actual fact Bach also made use of different types of oboe, e.g. the oboe d'amore in movement 5 and the Oboe da caccia in movement 7. The lowest string instrument is a violone, which served as a sort of double bass during the Baroque period. The orchestra would have been much smaller than the modern one, and the most obvious sign of the Baroque is the use of a continuo instrument, typically a keyboard instrument, and in this case the score requires both harpsichord and organ. The keyboard players provided chords to fill out the texture, and these were shown by the figured bass indications printed under the score, e.g. the first one, a 6/4 being a second inversion above the D in the bass, the following 4 indicating a suspension, and the 3 after that, the resolution.

The texture is also very characteristic of the music of the Baroque period as it is highly contrapuntal (although of course, Baroque composers could also write homophonically). The chorus parts come in like a fugal exposition, the subject being announced in the tenor with the orchestral bass parts providing a counterpoint. The subject itself is a highly ornamented, disguised version of the chorale melody – one of the most famous Reformation hymn tunes – and it lasts five bars. The answer appears in the alto and is heard with a counter-subject in the tenor, which is taken from the second line of the chorale. The chorale also appears separately in canon between oboes and violone. This combination of fugue and canon makes for a very powerful effect.

Examiner's points

In this essay, there is much AO3 information, notably the basic instrumentation details and the comments on texture. There were relatively few AO4 remarks. However, most of them connected with the peculiarly Baroque nature of the forces used and the comments on the background of the work.

The essay would have benefitted from AO4 discussion concerning the significance of the canon, comparable uses of similar textures in other works by Bach and some comparison with works by other composers.

The essay lacked a convincing conclusion and the remarks on figured bass were tending to stray more into the realms of harmony.

> **Evaluate Mozart's use of rhythm, metre and tempo, and melody in 'O zittre nicht' (bars 1–103) from *Die Zauberflöte*.**
>
> Relate your discussion to other relevant works. These may include set works, wider listening or other music.

Mark scheme

Before studying the mark scheme (indicative content) below, attempt the question yourself. You will find it useful to compare your answer with the mark scheme and the sample answer that follows.

Indicative content

Answers should show in equal proportions an ability to apply musical knowledge **[AO3]** and to offer evaluations and critical judgements about the music **[AO4]**:

Rhythm, metre and tempo

- The three sections of this recitative and aria are clearly differentiated in tempo, moving from Allegro maestoso to Larghetto and then to Allegro moderato
- Metres also change, moving from simple quadruple ($\frac{4}{4}$) to $\frac{3}{4}$ (Larghetto), then returning to $\frac{4}{4}$ for the final allegro. **[AO3]**

Characteristic rhythmic features include:

- Syncopation in the orchestral introduction **[AO3]**, imparting a sense of urgency **[AO4]**
- The 'free time' delivery in the recitative section **[AO3]**, producing the effect of heightened speech **[AO4]**
- Frequent dotted rhythms **[AO3]**
- Rapid flourishes, e.g. the triplet semiquavers in the Allegro moderato **[AO3]** for dramatic effect **[AO4]**
- Streams of semiquavers **[AO3]** to permit virtuoso display **[AO4]**
- Insertion of rests (e.g. bar 36) **[AO3]** to give impression of sighs. **[AO4]**

Melody

- Mozart employs a wide vocal range (over two octaves) **[AO3]** to underline the importance and power of this character **[AO4]**
- The last bar of the recitative contains a falling diminished 7th for pathos **[AO4]** and a typical closing formula of a falling 4th **[AO3]**
- Unusual phrase structure at the start of the aria, consisting of 3+3+2+2 bars **[AO3]** to convey a sense of uncertainty and pathos **[AO4]**
- Ornamentation and appoggiaturas **[AO3]** intensify expressive power **[AO4]**
- Sequence (bars 28–31) **[AO3]**
- Chromatic descent (bars 41–43) **[AO3]** for pathos **[AO4]**
- Melody in the Allegro moderato frequently contains rapidly moving scales **[AO3]**
- Word-setting involves a mix of syllabic, slurred quavers and melismas **[AO3]**, the latter often intensifying the dramatic effect. **[AO4]**

Historical context should be established, showing that this is an example of Singspiel, a type of German-language opera from the late 18th century/ Classical era. Comparison could be made with other Singspiel type works, e.g. Beethoven's *Fidelio* and Weber's *Der Freischütz*, as well as other operas and musical stage works. **[AO4]**

Sample answer

Mark this answer yourself, commenting on its good points and whether these satisfy AO3, AO4 or both. In addition, make a note of any aspects that could have been improved. Check your assessment against the examiner's comments that follow, after completing your marking.

The Magic Flute was one of the last works Mozart completed and is an example of Singspiel, a German language stage work with spoken dialogue, designed to appeal to a wider audience. In this piece, the Queen of the Night tells the hero, Tamino, he is to search for her daughter, Pamina, who has been kidnapped by Sarastro. It takes the form of a recitative and aria, and the recitative section is characterised by a speech rhythm style, resulting in a comparatively free rhythm. The vocal line contrasts strongly with the orchestral introduction, with its clearly defined pulse and use of syncopation.

The aria section is in two main parts, which contrast in both speed and time signature. The Larghetto is slower and has three beats to a bar, while the fast section returns to four beats to a bar, which had also been used at the start of the piece. This last section starts with triplet flourishes and eventually moves into fast-moving streams of semiquavers that require a singer who is a true virtuoso.

The virtuoso aspect is clear in other ways, notably the extremely wide range and very high 'coluratura' tessitura used towards the end. (This aspect is also evident in the Queen of the Night's second aria.) Mozart creates a sad mood in the recitative and Larghetto, partly through intervals like the falling diminished 7th at the end of the recitative and the minor mode used in the Larghetto. Here there is some irregular phrasing, with two sets of three bars to begin with. Later there are a number of broken up, grief-laden phrases with some sigh-like rests, as if the singer is overcome by her sadness. Other expressive features include appoggiaturas and ornamentation to intensify the effect and a descending chromatic line as the Queen describes the sorrow of her daughter. In contrast, her determination to get Tamino to rescue her comes over in the rapid scales and broken chord passages.

One of the key features of the Singspiel is spoken dialogue. Beethoven also used it in his opera Fidelio, but although Singspiel was a popular type of work, it was not so highly developed in the 19th century. Even in Germany, Wagner preferred to write continuous music. In fact it could be said that it was only with the musical that this type of stage music was widely used.

Examiner's points

In this essay, there are many correct AO3 observations on rhythmic aspects and melodic writing, and frequent attempts to explain the effects of these features in terms of creating an appropriate dramatic atmosphere, qualifying for AO4 credit.

There is understanding of the type of work used here **[AO4]**, although contrasts could have been made with other types of opera, which Mozart himself wrote. There was, however, some attempt to place the work within the German operatic tradition. The essay would have benefitted from a more focussed conclusion, and specific mention of later operas and musicals.

Instrumental music

Evaluate Vivaldi's use of texture and tonality in Movements I and II of his Concerto in D minor, Op. 3 No. 11.

Relate your discussion to other relevant works. These may include set works, wider listening or other music.

Mark scheme

Before studying the mark scheme (indicative content) below, attempt the question yourself. You will find it useful to compare your answer with the mark scheme and the sample answer that follows.

Indicative content

Answers should show in equal proportions an ability to apply musical knowledge **[AO3]** and to offer evaluations and critical judgements about the music **[AO4]**:

Tonality

- Tonality based on functional harmonic progressions and modulation
- Vivaldi modulates mainly to related keys:
  - A minor (movement II, bar 20)
  - G minor (movement II, bar 48)
  - F major (movement II, bar 52)
- Key of D minor established at the start of movement I, through the lengthy passage based
  on tonic broken chords
- Keys reinforced by cadences, e.g. perfect at movement I, bars 28–29
- Tierce de Picardie at movement II, bar 70 is 'cancelled out' at bar 73
- Circles of 5ths, e.g. at movement II, bars 5–7
- Dominant pedal at movement II, bars 58–69. **[AO3]**

Texture

- Movement I opens with a two-part canon at the distance of a crotchet beat, lengthening at bar 6 to one bar between imitations
- The passage at bar 20 in movement I is a cello melody with continuo accompaniment

- The Adagio opening to movement II is homophonic
- The following Allegro is fugal with:
  - Subject at bar 4
  - Counter-subject at bar 8
  - Answer at bar 8
- Concerto grosso contrasts are clear at e.g. movement II, bars 23–32, with the passage for the three string soloists with continuo
- Tasto solo bass at movement II, bar 58
- Homophony at movement II, bars 72–73. **[AO3]**

Historical context should be established, showing that this is an early 18th century/Baroque era work, in which contrasting of forces is of prime importance – as can be seen in concertos by Corelli, Handel and Bach. **[AO4]**

An attempt should be made to explain the effect of the devices listed above wherever possible. For example, variety is achieved through changes of key, dramatic effect of the curious treatment of the tierce de Picardie, the tension-building effect of the dominant pedal and the deliberate removal of continuo at this point, and the ingenious fusion of fugal textures with concerto principle. **[AO4]**

Reference should be made to other concerto works, especially those for groups of soloists, e.g. Beethoven's Triple Concerto, Brahms' Double Concerto. **[AO4]**

Sample answer

Mark this answer yourself, commenting on its good points and whether these satisfy AO3, AO4 or both. In addition, make a note of any aspects that could have been improved. Check your assessment against the examiner's comments that follow, after completing your marking.

The Vivaldi concerto is an example of a late-Baroque concerto grosso, with a small group of soloists (the concertino) contrasted with the main group of players (the ripieno). In this case, all the players, with the exception of the harpsichord continuo, play string instruments.

Vivaldi took up the genre as developed by composers such as Corelli and Torelli, and injected new energy into it with pounding, mechanical rhythms, and often broadening the solo groups to include woodwind instruments. He exerted a strong influence on J. S. Bach, who transcribed some of his concertos for other instruments – notably for organ, involving ingenious solutions to the problems of transferring string idioms to the keyboard.

Vivaldi was one of the first significant composers to use a tonal system built on functional harmonies. This system also permitted the use of modulation which in turn led to greater variety and also allowed the composition of longer structures. In this movement there are modulations to related keys, such as the dominant minor and relative major. Keys are established by cadences, e.g. the perfect cadence which appears at the end of the first fast section. Another way of establishing a key is the use of circle of 5ths, for example at the start of the fugue where the opening subject is supported by a progression of 7th chords with roots a 5th apart. Vivaldi also uses a prominent dominant pedal, the A in the bass parts, which runs for over ten bars towards the end of the second movement. It helps to prepare for the close on the tonic and builds up excitement. It also prepares for one of Vivaldi's most intriguing tricks with a Picardy 3rd four bars from the end, which is contradicted by the unexpected close on the tonic minor chord at the end.

As mentioned earlier, the work is a concerto grosso, and it has a concertino of two solo violins and cello. Given the limited resources at his disposal, Vivaldi was still able to introduce a wide range of textures including the two solo violins, unaccompanied, playing in close imitation at the start, followed by a passage for the solo cello accompanied by the continuo. The adagio which follows is built entirely on block chords (homophony), and there then follows a fugal exposition that leads on to a less fugal passage for the solo strings.

As said before, Vivaldi's influence on Bach is clear, and though most later concertos are typically for a single solo instrument, there are examples of concertos for groups of soloists, notably by Beethoven (the Triple Concerto for piano, violin and cello), Brahms (the Double Concerto for violin and cello) and Tippett (Triple Concerto for violin, viola and cello).

This shows how long-lasting the concerto form has proved to be.

Examiner's points

There were a number of sound musical observations under AO3, and here there were good solutions to the problem of locating devices in the possible absence of a score giving bar numbers.

A number of contextual points were made, referring to earlier composers, contemporaries and very much later works in the genre. However, only a limited number of AO4 observations were made. There could also have been more detailed information on the various forms of imitation. For example, the distance between parts at the start of the piece and terminology in the fugal section. The conclusion (final, single sentence) was rather insubstantial.

> **Evaluate Clara Schumann's use of structure and tonality in her Piano Trio in G minor, Op. 17, movement 1.**
>
> Relate your discussion to other relevant works. These may include set works, wider listening or other music.

Mark scheme

Before studying the mark scheme (indicative content) below, attempt the question yourself. You will find it useful to compare your answer with the mark scheme and the sample answer that follows.

Indicative content

Answers should show in equal proportions an ability to apply musical knowledge **[AO3]** and to offer evaluations and critical judgements about the music **[AO4]**:

The movement is in sonata form, and the various parts should be identified and located, along with details of keys used, as follows:

- Repeated exposition
- First subject in G minor
- Transition/bridge
- Second subject in B♭ major
- Development, mentioning keys, e.g. C minor, E♭, F minor etc.
- Recapitulation, starting with first subject in G minor
- Second subject in tonic major (G major)
- Coda. **[AO3]**

Historical context should be established, showing that this is a 19th century/ Romantic era treatment of a musical form, which originated in the 18th century/ Classical period, notably in the works of Haydn, Mozart and Beethoven. **[AO4]**

The expected modulation is used in the exposition and related keys are used in the development. There is use of the unrelated key of F minor and the repeat of the exposition is prepared by way of a transition back to the tonic. **[AO3]**

There is however nothing here that was not used in the works of late Classical composers (e.g. Beethoven), indicating a relatively conservative approach to the form. **[AO4]**

Dominant preparation is used at the end of the development **[AO3]**, paving the way for the recapitulation and heightening tension. **[AO4]**

Sample answer

Mark this answer yourself, commenting on its good points and whether these satisfy AO3, AO4 or both. In addition, make a note of any aspects that could have been improved. Check your assessment against the examiner's comments that follow, after completing your marking.

This work is in a typical Classical sonata form with exposition, development and recapitulation. It has a novel approach to keys, beginning and ending in Bb major, though it also has a passage in G major (you can tell because the key signature changes part way through).

Tonality is limited in this piece as it only requires a violin, a cello and a piano. It isn't possible to get much variety of sound because of this, and with only three instruments textures are bound to be a bit thin.

Simply by looking at the score provided, I can tell that Clara Schumann did her best though as the ranges used are much wider than expected. However, she could have used the pedal a bit more to get a thicker texture. She could also have used some more interesting effects, like pizzicato, to brighten things up.

It feels a very long movement, and this is partly because of the repeat of the opening bits.

Examiner's points

There is hardly anything here that would gain credit. At least the general remark about the structure being in sonata form is correct. It is also true that there is a passage in G major, though there is no indication of where in the movement this might be (i.e. second subject in recapitulation).

Simply listing component parts of a movement without location or further description (perhaps giving keys) is unlikely to gain credit. There were significant errors: e.g. Clara Schumann described as a Classical composer, key of Bb, tonality taken to refer to tone colour.

Music for film

Evaluate Portman's use of texture and tonality in 'Six Years Later'.

Relate your discussion to other relevant works. These may include set works, wider listening or other music.

Mark scheme

Before studying the mark scheme (indicative content) below, attempt the question yourself. You will find it useful to compare your answer with the mark scheme and the sample answer that follows.

Indicative content

Answers should show in equal proportions an ability to apply musical knowledge **[AO3]** and to offer evaluations and critical judgements about the music **[AO4]**:

Some contextual information should be provided, placing this film music in a line of scores for historical romances, in this case featuring late 18th/early 19th century aristocrats. It dates from 2008 but features a relatively small orchestra: in line with the composer's preferred methods, the orchestration employs only acoustic instruments. Although dealing with 18th century events, Portman avoids pastiche, but perhaps hints at earlier times and an English background through the use of modality. **[AO4]**

Texture

- Melody-dominated homophony throughout
- Waltz accompaniment, with single/octave bass notes on the first quaver of each three and chords on second and third quavers
- Occasional additional patterns in strings and horns
- On repeat, texture expanded with chords in upper parts
- Waltz dies out with single sustained bass note
- The second part refers to materials of the Opening with pedal in bass and accompaniment of running quavers (tonic and dominant) and off-beat chords
- Texture reduced at the close to two parts consisting of sustained bass and quavers figure. **[AO3]**

Tonality

- Tonality is D mixolydian (C♯ is replaced with a C♮)
- There is no modulation
- Some cadences, e.g. a modal perfect cadence at the close
- Tonality established by tonic pedals. **[AO3]**

AO4 credit will be available for discussion of how the above features contribute to the creation of an appropriate atmosphere. Further credit will be earned through reference to incidental music for other historical films, e.g. adaptations of Jane Austen novels, *Shakespeare in Love*, *Aleksander Nevsky*.

Sample answer

Mark this answer yourself, commenting on its good points and whether these satisfy AO3, AO4 or both. In addition, make a note of any aspects that could have been improved. Check your assessment against the examiner's comments that follow, after completing your marking.

Portman's score for The Duchess is delicate in the way it supports most of the action, an account of the career of Georgina Cavendish, the Duchess of Devonshire. In attempting to recreate an appropriate late 18th century atmosphere, Portman uses music by Haydn and Beethoven at some points, but the original music she supplied avoids pastiche.

The mood created in 'Six Years Later' is clearly cheerful, and this feeling is established in the waltz which opens this cue. The textures throughout are uncomplicated – essentially melody-dominated homophony or melody and accompaniment, and would present no challenges to the listener. In fact the waltz is extremely simple, the only variations on the melody and accompaniment approach being the short fragments, which sometimes appear in the inner parts as well as the use of a larger band on the repeat of the theme with sustained chords in the upper parts. The waltz section fades out with just rhythmic patterns and a final long sustained note in the bass.

The second part is a modified repeat of the music of the opening cue, and like with the opening there is use of a pedal and off-beat chords in the middle part of the texture. Added to this, there is a constant quaver pattern, moving between tonic and dominant. The texture is reduced towards the end to two parts, one a long sustained bass note, and the other the quaver pattern.

Tonality is also straightforward and designed not to upset listeners. The cue is clearly meant to sound old-fashioned English, and so modal features are employed. Whether this is stylistically correct is another matter as English art music of the late 18th century and early 19th, like that of continental classical composers, was strictly functional. Here, however, the D major tonality is subjected to mixolydian twists, i.e. the C# is replaced with C naturals. This modal element even infects the harmonies, so that besides the D major tonic chords, the dominant chord is A minor, sometimes with 7th, rather than major. As the harmony is limited mainly to these two chords, it is impossible to create much variety in the tonal scheme. There is no modulation, and the alternation between these chords can only produce imperfect and perfect cadences, as at the end. The key of D is further emphasised by the use of the tonic pedals and the frequent broken chord patterns in the inner parts.

Examiner's points

Unsurprisingly, the student here clearly found it difficult to find much to say about this cue, but made the best of a difficult situation, offering a significant amount of AO3 information. There is also some basic context and useful discussion regarding the use of modality, which would gain credit under AO4. The essay would, however, have benefitted from a conclusion and some attempt to compare this film score with others.

> **Evaluate Elfman's use of melody and harmony in 'Rise and Fall from Grace'.**
>
> Relate your discussion to other relevant works. These may include set works, wider listening or other music.

Mark scheme

Before studying the mark scheme (indicative content) below, attempt the question yourself. You will find it useful to compare your answer with the mark scheme and the sample answer that follows.

Indicative content

Answers should show in equal proportions an ability to apply musical knowledge **[AO3]** and to offer evaluations and critical judgements about the music **[AO4]**:

Some contextual information should be provided, placing this film music in a line of scores for blockbuster movies, in this case featuring comic book characters in a fantasy adventure story. It is a late-20th-century work, featuring a full orchestra with a number of extra parts. The music is intended to be both approachable and arresting. It broadly follows methods (leitmotif, underscoring) that date as far back as the 1930s in film music, and in the case of leitmotif, go back to Wagner. **[AO4]**

Melody

- Elfman uses a system of leitmotifs associated with the main characters
- The most famous one is the Batman motif, but this cue is based almost entirely on the ones associated with the Penguin
- Motifs are subjected to variation and transformation, depending on the demands of the dramatic situation
- The first Penguin motif consists of four notes, moving around the initial note by step
- The second motif, in minor mode, after rising a minor 3rd moves by step
- It is initially heard in long notes/minims
- The first motif is presented in the form of a waltz
- Other features include:
  - Broken chord figures
  - Appoggiaturas.

Harmony

- Functional language, with frequent cadences **[AO3]** reflecting the music's popular style **[AO4]**
- Dominant pedal (near the start, bars 4–11) **[AO3]**, creating suspense **[AO4]**
- Diminished 7th (section following the waltz passage, bar 42) **[AO3]**
- Augmented triad (very close to the end, bar 51) **[AO3]**, contributing to the sinister atmosphere **[AO4]**
- Augmented 6th chord (towards the end, bar 45) **[AO3]**, contributing to the sinister atmosphere **[AO4]**
- Whole-tone chords (final section, bars 50–52) **[AO3]** with destabilising effect **[AO4]**
- Sudden, unexpected close on C (effect of tierce de Picardie) **[AO3]**, bringing sense of resolution **[AO4]**.

Sample answer

Mark this answer yourself, commenting on its good points and whether these satisfy AO3, AO4 or both. In addition, make a note of any aspects which could have been improved. Check your assessment against the examiner's comments that follow, after completing your marking.

Batman Returns was released in 1992 and was clearly intended to be a popular blockbuster aimed at a wide audience. Danny Elfman was commissioned to write the music as he was a well-established composer of incidental music in a popular style; his best known work being the music for The Simpsons. Part of the appeal of the film lay in its epic proportions and spectacular effects, and the music had to match that. As a result, the orchestration drew on a huge array of resources including organ, children's choir, synthesiser, celeste, piano, accordion, a large percussion section with xylophone, marimba, temple blocks, sleighbells, tam-tam and cymbals, as well as a large symphony orchestra.

The melody and harmony play their part in creating a popular, approachable style. To underline the developing drama, Elfman used a system of recurring themes or motifs which were frequently varied as the situation required in a manner reminiscent of earlier operas, e.g. those by Wagner with its systems of leitmotifs representing characters, objects and ideas. In this score, the most famous is the Batman motif, heard right at the start of 'Birth of the

Penguin Part I' and throughout 'Birth of a Penguin Part II' and 'Batman vs the Circus'. Other important motifs are linked to the Penguin, and it is these that are most used in 'Rise and Fall from Grace'. The four-note motif that ran through 'Birth of a Penguin Part I', moving around by step, appears in the bass instruments, so contrasting with the high string writing. The second motif follows on, again in lower instruments and sounds menacing with its drawn-out notes. One of the most striking variations occurs with a sinister waltz section where the original Penguin motif supplies the bass to the accordion's waltz rhythms. The rest of the movement involves a significant amount of broken chord figuration, and towards the end there is a series of appoggiaturas.

The harmonic language is simple and direct and is often functional with cadences, such as the imperfect cadences that frequently occur in the first part and add to the continuity here. This movement, however, illustrates particularly well the way Elfman combines different harmonic features, e.g. the dominant pedal at the start, the triadic harmony in the waltz, the diminished 7ths, chromatic chords (augmented 6th), augmented triad and whole-tone harmony, before finishing with a sudden C major chord.

Elfman has said that a number of 20th century composers, including Bartók, Glass, Ravel and Stravinsky have influenced him strongly, and this is shown in the various extracts from Batman Returns, which combine advanced techniques with a basically popular style to exciting effect.

Examiner's points

This essay included a significant amount of AO3 information with melodic material sufficiently well located. A number of harmonic devices were listed, but not all were located, and in general there was little attempt to relate the device to the effect the music might have created in the viewer. There was some useful AO4 discussion of the nature of Elfman's approach, although the first paragraph included an unnecessarily lengthy list of instruments used.

Popular music and jazz

Evaluate Pine's use of melody and rhythm in 'Inner state (of mind)'.

Relate your discussion to other relevant works. These may include set works, wider listening or other music.

Mark scheme

Before studying the mark scheme (indicative content) below, attempt the question yourself. You will find it useful to compare your answer with the mark scheme and the sample answer that follows.

Indicative content

Answers should show in equal proportions an ability to apply musical knowledge **[AO3]** and to offer evaluations and critical judgements about the music **[AO4]**:

AO4 credit will be awarded for establishing Pine's place in the development of jazz and the various strands making up his approach that can be heard in this piece. Reference should be made to the music of other jazz composers.

Tempo, metre and rhythm

- 'Inner state (of mind)' is in a brisk quadruple throughout.
- Typical rhythmic features include:
  - Syncopation (e.g. bar 2)
  - Dotted rhythms (bar 11)
  - Lombardic rhythm/Scotch snap (bar 75)
  - Irregular groupings, e.g. quintuplet in instrumental
  - Long note (with trill) at the end. **[AO3]**

Melody

This number is characterised by:

- Pentatonicism (bars 1–2)
- Blue notes (first note in tenor sax, at bar 2)

- Chromaticism (instrumental, e.g. bar 100 with ornamented chromatic descent outlined at start of each beat)
- Borrowing of melody from Gershwin's 'Summertime' from *Porgy and Bess*
- Scat singing ('Inner state', bars 52-53)
- Melismas (e.g. 'mankind')
- Relatively narrow range
- Repetition of short figures (see passage near end)
- Frequent ornamentation, e.g.
  - Acciaccaturas (opening sax solo)
  - Trill at close
  - Sliding up to pitch (start of sax solo)
  - Glissandos (instrumental near end, bars 91-93) **[AO3]**

Sample answer

Mark this answer yourself, commenting on its good points and whether these satisfy AO3, AO4 or both. In addition, make a note of any aspects that could have been improved. Check your assessment against the examiner's comments that follow, after completing your marking.

In 'Inner state (of mind)', a piece of contemporary jazz, Pine uses a number of techniques that clearly show the influences of not only a number of earlier jazz musicians but also more recent rappers.

In terms of rhythm, metre and tempo, the piece is quick, and has four beats to a bar. Rhythmic devices are typical of the style, with syncopation, various sorts of dotted rhythm.

Melodically it is more interesting with references to 'Summertime' from Gershwin's Porgy and Bess. It is as well to draw a line between what happens in the vocal parts and the tenor sax part. The Gershwin quote is relatively narrow in range, and is in C minor. The other recurring motif, heard right at the start of 'Inner state (of mind)' is a rising pentatonic idea. Other features of the vocal parts include the scat singing and the rap materials.

The instrumentals are more varied and have

• Chromatic passages

• Blue notes

• Ornamentation

• Slides

• A very long glissando, which allows Pine to show off his phenomenal instrumental skills.

Examiner's points

The response was at best limited. The opening point about contemporary jazz was undeveloped, and apart from mentioning Gershwin, there was no significant attempt to refer to other composers.

There was, however, some attempt to outline rhythmic and melodic features. Nevertheless, these references were vague, as there were no locations or descriptions which would have served to support the basic point. The use of bullet points should be avoided, and their use here would affect the assessment adversely.

Evaluate harmony and tonality and structure in Kate Bush's 'Cloudbusting'.

Relate your discussion to other relevant works. These may include set works, wider listening or other music.

Mark scheme

Before studying the mark scheme (indicative content) below, attempt the question yourself. You will find it useful to compare your answer with the mark scheme and the sample answer that follows.

Indicative content

Answers should show in equal proportions an ability to apply musical knowledge **[AO3]** and to offer evaluations and critical judgements about the music **[AO4]**:

AO4 credit will be awarded for establishing contributing elements in the formation of Bush's style, the background behind the song under discussion and attempts to make relevant links with the music of other composers.

Harmony

- A limited number of dissonant added-note chords are frequently employed (C♯m⁷ – B major with added 9th – A major with added 9th and 6th, and the occasional G♯ minor chord with added 4th) **[AO3]**, underlining the mechanical effect created by other elements of the song **[AO4]**
- The limited chord choice is reminiscent of that of the Beatles' song 'Eleanor Rigby' **[AO4]**
- All chords contain both B and C♯ **[AO3]**
- Harmonic rhythm is varied, e.g. at the opening the C♯ and B chords have two beats, whereas at bar 95, chords are allotted four beats. **[AO3]**

Tonality and structure

- C♯ minor
- No modulation
- Verse and chorus pattern with instrumentals:

  Verse – Bridge – Chorus (twice)

  Instrumental – Chorus

  Instrumental and coda with chorus material **[AO3]**

Sample answer

Mark this answer yourself, commenting on its good points and whether these satisfy AO3, AO4 or both. In addition, make a note of any aspects which could have been improved. Check your assessment against the examiner's comments that follow, after completing your marking.

The Hounds of Love album consists of two main sections, originally dictated by the album's release on 12" vinyl. The first side consisted of a number of progressive rock pieces, and the second side was a sort of concept collection of songs, devoted to the story of a girl drowning. It took as its inspiration Tennyson's Poem 'The Holy Grail' from the cycle Idylls of the King about King Arthur. In contrast the song 'Cloudbusting' was suggested by A Book of Dreams by Peter Reich. It has to do with the psychologist Wilhelm Reich, who had fled Nazi-dominated Europe and his eccentric attempts to make rain by pointing a machine, the cloudbuster, at the sky. There are also references to Reich's arrest and imprisonment by the American authorities for trying to sell 'quack' contraptions for curing mental illness and cancer.

The harmony of the song is based on a restricted range of chords, which produces a rather machine-like effect. These are hammered out in a rather mechanical way, and when combined with the instrumentation, and especially the string sextet, it has an alienating effect like the harmony and scoring of 'Eleanor Rigby' by the Beatles. The chords are dissonant, so underlining the rather despairing feel of the song. All the chords used contain both B and C#, e.g. the C# minor 7th and the B major with added 9th. The rate of harmonic change is varied so that the opening chords have two beats, whereas when they occur later, with hammering rhythms in addition, they have four beats.

The structure of the song is very typical of popular music as it is a verse, bridge and chorus layout with instrumentals appearing from time to time. The rather grim atmosphere is emphasised by the C# minor tonality and the absence of modulation.

Examiner's points

There were useful introductory comments here on *Hounds of Love* and the story lying behind 'Cloudbusting'. The link with 'Eleanor Rigby' was, however, the only reference to other works. Comments on the harmony were valid, as were those on structure and tonality, although the overall scheme of the song could have been described in greater detail.

Fusions

Evaluate Debussy's use of harmony and tonality in 'Pagodes'.

Relate your discussion to other relevant works. These may include set works, wider listening or other music.

Mark scheme

Before studying the mark scheme (indicative content) below, attempt the question yourself. You will find it useful to compare your answer with the mark scheme and the sample answer that follow.

Indicative content

Answers should show in equal proportions an ability to apply musical knowledge **[AO3]** and to offer evaluations and critical judgements about the music **[AO4]**:

AO4 credit will be awarded for establishing historical context and stylistic features that indicate that this is an impressionistic work. Other composers of the time should be mentioned, especially in connection with the use of non-European content.

Harmony

The harmony of 'Pagodes' is strongly affected by the work's melodic pentatonicism, which was influenced by gamelan music. It is marked by:

- Its static quality
- Avoidance of functional progressions
- Slow harmonic rhythm
- 'Changing background' approach, i.e. changing harmonisations of the same melody
- The added 6th (B–D♯–F♯–G♯) at the start
- Other prominent landmarks include:
  - Extended chords, e.g. B^{13} (bar 7)
  - Diminished triad (bar 16^2)
  - Colouristic major 2nd, heard in isolation at the start of the central section
  - Pentatonic harmonisation at bar 37, with parallelism and open 5th chords. **[AO3]**

Tonality

- The first and last sections are based on B major, though Debussy avoids simple triads, preferring added chords, e.g. the 6th at the start
- The central passage moves into the region of F# major/D# minor. **[AO4]**

Sample answer

Mark this answer yourself, commenting on its good points and whether these satisfy AO3, AO4 or both. In addition, make a note of any aspects that could have been improved. Check your assessment against the examiner's comments that follow, after completing your marking.

In 'Pagodes', Debussy's piano writing went in a new direction. He had already adopted a sort of impressionistic style in some of his early orchestral works, e.g. Prélude à l'après-midi d'un faune and Nocturnes, both dating from the previous decade. It is known that the development of this style may have been suggested by Ravel's piano piece, Jeux d'eau, which appeared the year before 'Pagodes', i.e. 1902. Ravel's piece is marked by a colouristic use of the keyboard, with use of extreme ranges and pedal to produce haze effects.

The other important influence on Debussy in this piece is the Javanese gamelan, which he first heard at the Paris World Exhibition of 1889. It is interesting to note that with regard to harmony Debussy once said that gamelan music made tonic and dominant 'seem like ghosts'. He seems to have carried that into effect in 'Pagodes', because here there is no use of functional harmony with cadences built on tonic and dominant chords. In fact the harmonic scheme is slow-moving and often seems to freeze up on one chord, e.g. the B major chord with added G# which appears at the opening. When they occur, harmonic changes are often very slight, supporting the same melody with varied harmonies, rather like the music of some Russian composers whose music Debussy admired.

The pentatonicism associated with Javanese and Balinese music also had some impact on the harmony with chords which are put together from notes in the pentatonic scale often with novel effect. Other typical Debussy devices are the parallel structures, e.g. the 5ths which clearly have an oriental sound to them.

Because there is no functional harmony, tonality is not so important a feature in the structuring of this piece. It starts and ends in B major, and it has a contrasting section in the middle, which seems to touch on minor keys and perhaps has a touch of the whole-tone scale about it.

This piece paved the way for other explorations of oriental music, such as Messiaen, e.g. Turangalîla Symphony.

Examiner's points

This essay was well supplied with AO4 context and references to works by other composers. It included valid comments on tonality and harmony, though it would have been possible to mention other harmonic features.

> **Evaluate sonority and texture in La Familia Valera Miranda's 'Se quema la chumbambá' and 'Allá va candela'.**
>
> Relate your discussion to other relevant works. These may include set works, wider listening or other music.

Mark scheme

Before studying the mark scheme (indicative content) below, attempt the question yourself. You will find it useful to compare your answer with the mark scheme and the sample answer that follows.

Indicative content

Answers should show in equal proportions an ability to apply musical knowledge **[AO3]** and to offer evaluations and critical judgements about the music **[AO4]**:

Credit will be awarded for establishing historical context, background and stylistic features which indicate that these songs are examples of Cuban music. Other works by composers influenced by music of this region or South America in general should be mentioned.

Sonority

- Performing forces in both numbers are:
  - Solo male voice (Pregón) and male-voice chorus (Coro)
  - Cuatro, a four-course guitar-like instrument (with eight strings)
  - Guitar
  - Plucked double bass
  - Maracas, claves and bongo.

  [AO3, with AO4 credit for commenting on the function or role of each performer.]

Texture

- Melody-dominated homophony predominates in both songs
- The Coro in 'Se quema' is homophonic (homorhythmic), with the two parts singing in 3rds, 6ths, diminished 5ths and perfect 4ths
- In 'Allá va candela', the Coro is confined to interjections of two notes in octaves
- Monophony (cuatro) can be heard at the opening of both songs
- The cuatro solos in both songs involve some multi-stopping **[AO3]** for display. **[AO4]**

Sample answer

Mark this answer yourself, commenting on its good points and whether these satisfy AO3, AO4 or both. In addition, make a note of any aspects that could have been improved. Check your assessment against the examiner's comments that follow, after completing your marking.

Resources and resulting sonorities are typical of the music of Cuba. The group in question comes from the Eastern region of the island, and the performers have long-established connections with nationalists and freedom-fighters over the last century and a half. Their music often reflects their work as farmers, e.g. 'Se quema la chumbambá' refers to the burning of sugar cane on the land. Other songs are more general in subject matter, with 'Allá va candela' being about one member of the group falling in love.

Both songs were composed or improvised at musical sessions in the early years of the last century, and they are cast in typical forms of Cuban music, e.g. son in the case of 'Se quema la chumbambá' and bolero-son in 'Allá va candela'. The son is a call and response type of song, and often employs typical son-claves rhythmic patterns. The general style of both numbers is a fusion of Afro-Cuban with Spanish elements, the Spanish for a long time being the rulers of the island. The so-called bolero is interesting because its rhythmic scheme is quite different from the sort of triple time dance patterns associated with the European version, being in duple time. It is usually more song-like than the son. In actual fact, this song is only a bolero for the opening section, and turns into a son part-way through.

The Afro-Cuban elements, mentioned above, are most evident in the percussion instruments used in both songs, chiefly maracas, bongos and claves. Once established these instruments keep to the same patterns all the way through, and prominent among them is the son-clave rhythm with three notes in one bar and two notes in the next (in 'Se quema' only). Obviously, these instruments keep the beat throughout. Other accompaniment instruments are the double bass, inherited from Spanish music. This instrument is plucked and provides an essential harmonic support, i.e. tonic and dominant for the most part, rarely going beyond basic chords. The cuatro also has a prominent solo in both songs, for display purposes. Chords are provided on the cuatro, a guitar-like instrument with four double courses. The remaining sonorities are vocal, with a solo voice answered by the two-part coro (chorus).

Moving on to texture, both songs are essentially homophonic, with clearly defined melody and accompaniment. Antiphony is especially prominent in 'Se quema', which consists of a constant alternation between solo voice and the coro. There are brief passages of monophony at the start of both songs.

Examiner's points

It seems that the writer here was distracted from the given brief as, given the limited time available for producing an essay, it was only well into the essay that the subjects of sonority and texture were addressed. It is true that there was some useful background and context, but it may have been more helpful to focus on additional aspects of sonority and texture, and also to have given particulars of other works revealing Latin-American features.

New directions

Evaluate rhythm and texture in the first of Cage's Three Dances for two prepared pianos.

Relate your discussion to other relevant works. These may include set works, wider listening or other music.

Mark scheme

Before studying the mark scheme (indicative content) below, attempt the question yourself. You will find it useful to compare your answer with the mark scheme and the sample answer that follows.

Indicative content

Answers should show in equal proportions an ability to apply musical knowledge **[AO3]** and to offer evaluations and critical judgements about the music **[AO4]**:

Credit will be awarded for establishing historical context, circumstances of composition and specific stylistic features that indicate that this work was by Cage and his contemporaries. Other avant-garde works should be mentioned. **[AO3/4]**

Texture

- Texture is mainly contrapuntal, with the two piano parts frequently working independently
- Generally, a two-part texture is used for each piano
- Other features to note include:
    - Monophony (bar 14 in phrase 5)
    - A sort of melody-dominated homophony (phrase 38)
    - Homorhythm (phrase 7) **[AO3]**

Tempo, metre and rhythm

- Tempo is a fast duple time ($\frac{2}{2}$) throughout, at 88 minims per minute
- Note values are largely quavers and crotchets
- Duple metre is disrupted through cross-rhythms, mainly groupings of three quavers at a time (see opening, piano 1)

- Working against piano 1's opening rhythm is a steady crotchet pattern in piano 2, left hand, with off-beat quavers in the right hand
- Notice, however, that the left-hand figure in piano 2 consists of a seven crotchet ostinato, also working against the written duple time. **[AO3]**

Sample answer

Mark this answer yourself, commenting on its good points and whether these satisfy AO3, AO4 or both. In addition, make a note of any aspects which could have been improved. Check your assessment against the examiner's comments that follow, after completing your marking.

Cage was one of the most interesting of the avant-garde composers in the 20th century, and his work certainly took music in a new direction. In this case, the novel aspects of his composition stemmed from his work as the provider of musical accompaniments to a dance company, run by Merce Cunningham. The dancers had only a limited space in which to work, and it was not possible for Cage to use the percussion instruments he had originally proposed to use. He solved the problem of producing a percussive sound by 'preparing' the piano, that is by modifying the piano's sounds by inserting various objects between the strings. Because it was primarily dance music, the rhythmic element was extremely important, and in fact pitch was almost irrelevant, and impossible to predict from one performance to the next.

In fact it could be said that, apart from the sonorities arising from the piano's preparation, texture and rhythm were the only musical elements that were relevant: melody and harmony were unpredictable or non-existent, and tonality was impossible to organise. At the same time, texture and rhythm are the two elements which it is possible to understand in traditional terms.

In the case of texture, the music is mainly contrapuntal, with a two-part texture on each piano working independently. This is the element that contributes to the sense of teeming activity created by the music. There are sometimes other types of texture like a type of melody-dominated homophony and even homorhythm when all the parts are heard working together. There is also some fleeting single-line writing.

The music is fast and furious, moving at a brisk 88 minims per minute, with two minims to the bar. The constant use of quavers and crotchets also contributes to the frantic feel of this piece. This sensation is also underlined by the regular feeling of having parts working at odds with each other. For example, the grouping of quavers in threes working across the beat and the irregular seven-crotchet pattern in the bass part.

Frantic as this music is, it is nothing like as complicated as some of Cage's macro-microcosmic schemes (Sonatas and Interludes). In the end, there is still nothing as complex as Stravinsky's Rite of Spring (the sacrificial dance) or Messiaen's use of recurring rhythmic durations (Chronochromie).

Examiner's points

There is good background information with reference to circumstances of composition. There is also a good understanding of the effects of preparation on traditional musical elements, and the extent to which they can be experienced.

There was some attempt to relate the various rhythmic and textural features to the overall impression created by the music, although more could have been said in both areas. There was mention of two works by other composers, but no discussion as to how they might compare with Cage's work.

> **Evaluate Kaija Saariaho's use of melody and structure in *Petals*.**
>
> Relate your discussion to other relevant works. These may include set works, wider listening or other music.

Mark scheme

Before studying the mark scheme (indicative content) below, attempt the question yourself. You will find it useful to compare your answer with the mark scheme and the sample answer that follows.

Indicative content

Answers should show in equal proportions an ability to apply musical knowledge [AO3] and to offer evaluations and critical judgements about the music [AO4].

Credit will be awarded for establishing historical context, with reference to other composers, and discussion of technological issues where relevant **[AO4]**.

Melody

- Melodic content is generally confined to the faster moving sections as opposed to the more colouristic 'Lento' passages
- In stave 4 the melodic line contains quarter tones and glissandos
- Stave 10 onwards has more obvious melodic content, with leaps of major 7th and augmented 4th **[AO3]** producing expressive effect **[AO4]**
- Repeated note figuration (stave 11)
- Short descending figures (stave 11) **[AO3]** give sense of structure **[AO4]**
- Ornamentation at stave 23 includes striking use of glissandos rising alternately to C♯ and F♯, supported by low pedal (open string) Cs **[AO3]**, producing a sense of regularity and structural order **[AO4]**
- The section culminates with a glissando to the highest pitch available (stave 27) **[AO3]** as climax. **[AO4]**

Structure

- Single continuous movement
- Some brief repetition of 'motifs' (glissando figures from stave 23) **[AO3]** gives sense of order **[AO4]**
- The piece alternates 'fragile colouristic passages' with 'more energetic events' **[AO3]** giving the listener a clear sense of direction **[AO4]**
- There are seven sections, alternating between 'Lento' passages and faster moving passages **[AO3]**
- The climax comes in section 6 **[AO3]**, giving sense of purpose to the whole. **[AO4]**

Sample answer

Mark this answer yourself, commenting on its good points and whether these satisfy AO3, AO4 or both. In addition, make a note of any aspects which could have been improved. Check your assessment against the examiner's comments that follow, after completing your marking.

On the face of it, it may seem strange to talk of melody and structure in the case of a piece such as this, but though couched in an avant-garde form, these two elements are clearly discernable. It is true that the cello sound is subjected to various electronic transformations in performance, though there is a note on the score stating that such electronic treatment is not compulsory.

It is probably more useful to deal with structure first. Petals is one continuous movement in which colouristic passages in slow tempo are alternated with faster, more animated sections. The slow tempo sections are those in which the electronic enhancements come most noticeably into play, while the faster parts, though still subjected to reverb and the effects of the harmoniser, are more clearly melodic. There are seven sections altogether, with the main climax occurring in the sixth ('poco impetuoso', staves 17 to 27).

As stated above, the slower passages are not so obviously melodic, and it is only with the energico part that the first melodic stirrings can be detected. These take the form of glissandos and quarter-tone elements. Pronounced melodic elements come into play properly in the second faster moving passage, where we hear some clearly defined intervals, some quite wide such as the 6th in stave 10 and the major 7th in stave 12. The rhythms here are more clearly defined (the lento passages are extremely free and aleatoric), notably in the rapid repeated note figures. Other melodic features occurring later in the piece include dramatic glissandos reaching up to C# and F# in alternation. The climax of the piece comes with a glissando reaching the highest note the soloist can manage to play.

Clear indications are given at the start of the score regarding notation and the effects intended, including bow pressure, types of glissando and microtones. Many of these effects can be seen in other contemporary pieces, notably the aleatoric scores of Lutosławski. He also composed a cello concerto that pushed the bounds of the instrument's technique and styles of writing, though without resorting to electronic devices.

Examiner's points

The essay started well with a useful opening gambit. The decision to start with structure was also a good idea, as it could make discussion of the melodic elements and their location more straightforward.

There was a lot of relevant basic information, and some attempt to show how the various melodic and structural features contributed to the impact of the work. There was clearly some understanding of notation and electronic modification, although reference to other music was rather cursory.

Acciaccatura. A very short ornamental note played before a principal melodic note, written or printed as ♪

Additive rhythm. Where a bar has beats of unequal length, or where unequal short rhythmic sets are grouped together to form a longer rhythmic pattern.

Aeolian mode. A scale that uses the following pattern of tones (T) and semitones (s): T–s–T–T–s–T–T. When starting on A, it consists of all the white notes within one octave on a keyboard.

Alberti bass. A particular type of broken chord pattern often found in classical keyboard music with three pitches heard in the order low-high-middle-high, e.g. C–G–E–G.

Aleatoric. Music that contains an element of chance or choice on the part of the performer, meaning that its exact course cannot be predicted until it is performed. Music of this kind can also be called 'indeterminate'.

Anacrusis. Note or notes preceding the first beat of a piece or phrase.

Angular. When applied to melody, the presence of wide leaps.

Anthem. A type of church music for choir, often accompanied by organ, and occasionally by larger forces. An anthem usually has English words (often from the Bible).

Antiphony. Performance by different singers/instrumentalists in alternation. Often – but not always – the different groups perform similar material.

Appoggiatura. A non-chord note that sounds on the beat as a dissonance and then resolves by step (up or down) to the main chord note. The dissonant note is not 'prepared' as a suspension is. Although appoggiaturas are normally approached by leap, accented passing notes that are particularly long and/or prominent are often described as appoggiaturas, even though they are approached by step. Sometimes an appoggiatura, especially in the Classical period, is indicated by a note in small type, followed by its resolution printed at normal size.

Arco. A direction to bow notes on a string instrument.

Aria. A song (usually from an **opera**, oratorio or **cantata**) for solo voice, plus accompaniment for orchestra or, sometimes in Baroque times, for smaller forces, even just **continuo**. An aria often provides a character in an opera with the opportunity to reflect at length on their emotional state.

Articulation. The manner in which a series of notes are played with regards to their separation or connection – for example, staccato (separated) or legato (connected).

Atonal. Atonal music avoids keys or modes; that is, no pitch stands out consistently in the way that the tonic does in tonal music.

Augmentation. The lengthening of the rhythmic values of a previously-heard melody (e.g. where ♩♫ has become 𝅗𝅥 ♩♩).

Augmented triad. A three-note chord in which the interval between successive notes is a major 3rd; for example, the chord D–F♯–A♯.

Augmented 6th chord. A chromatic chord which in root position spans the interval of an augmented 6th, e.g. A♭–F♯.

Auxiliary note. A type of passing note that moves away and then returns to the main beat note by step, e.g. D-C-D or G-A-G.

Bebop. A style of jazz that developed in the 1940s from swing. More complex and less easy to dance to, it was characterised by **improvisation**, fast tempos, irregular phrase lengths and a greater emphasis on the rhythm section.

Binary form. A structure consisting of two sections, the first of which closes in a related key and the second in the tonic. This structure was frequently used by Baroque composers, e.g. in dance movements.

Bitonal. Music that uses two different keys simultaneously.

Broken chord. The performing of the notes of a chord one after another instead of simultaneously.

Cadence. A pair of chords signifying the end of a phrase in tonal music. Cadences are of several types, of which perfect and imperfect are by far the most common. *See also* **Imperfect cadence**, **Interrupted cadence**, **Perfect cadence**, **Plagal cadence** and **Phrygian cadence**.

Cadential 6-4. Chord Ic, preceding chord V or V^7 in a perfect or imperfect cadence.

Canon. A strict form of **imitation**, in which each successive part repeats exactly the music of the first part.

Cantata. Most commonly a work for voice(s) and instruments in several movements, with **aria**(s), **recitative**(s) and chorus(es). A cantata can be sacred or secular.

Chorale. A German hymn of the kind sung in the Lutheran (Protestant) church in the time of J. S. Bach. The word 'chorale' can refer to the words only, to the associated melody only, or to the whole hymn. Chorale melodies are largely stepwise (or **conjunct**); their harmonisation has long featured in advanced music courses.

Chordal. A form of homophony in which all the parts move together in the same or very similar rhythm. The term **homorhythmic** (literally 'same rhythm') is sometimes used instead.

Chromatic. A chromatic note is one that does not belong to the scale of the key currently in use. For example, in D major the notes G♯ and C♮ are chromatic. Music that is chromatic contains many chromatic notes.

Circle of 5ths. A harmonic progression in which the roots of the chords move by descending 5ths (and/or ascending 4ths), e.g. B–E–A–D–G–C etc.

Coda. A concluding section of a movement.

Compound time. A metre in which the main beat is subdivided into three equal portions, as opposed to two equal portions in simple time.

Concerto. Most commonly, a work for a soloist with orchestra. In many concertos the solo instrument is a piano or violin. Occasionally there may be two soloists (a double concerto) or even three (a triple concerto). (In the 17th century the term was used more widely, and was applied originally to a work in which voices and instruments, with more or less independent parts, collaborated in a manner that was new at the time.) *See also* **Concerto grosso**.

Concerto grosso. A type of concerto, most common in the late Baroque period, in which three (or occasionally more) soloists, known as the 'concertino', are contrasted with the sound of a larger group of mainly string instruments, known as the 'ripieno'.

Conjunct. Melodic movement by step rather than by leap. Opposite of **disjunct**.

Continuo. Short for 'basso continuo', the continuo instruments form the accompaniment in Baroque music. It may include instruments such as the harpsichord (capable of playing full harmony) and a cello or bassoon reinforcing the bass line.

Contrapuntal. Adjective to describe music that uses **counterpoint**.

Counterpoint. Counterpoint involves two or more melodic lines (usually rhythmically contrasted), each significant in itself, which are played or sung together at the same time. The term polyphonic is often used as a synonym for contrapuntal.

Countersubject. In a fugue, the melodic material that is heard in counterpoint with the answer.

Course. Two or more adjacent strings on an instrument that are intended to be played as a single string.

Cross rhythm. The use of two or more very different rhythms simultaneously in different parts. One rhythm may imply one metre (or time signature), while another implies a different one.

Cue. This term refers to a particular portion of music intended for inclusion at a specific point of a film.

Development. The central part of a **sonata form** movement between the **exposition** and the recapitulation, containing a working-out of ideas already heard in the exposition.

Dialogue. When two or more instruments or voices have a musical 'conversation', with the individual parts responding to one another.

Diatonic. Using notes that belong to the current key. A diatonic note is one that belongs to the scale of the key currently in use. For example, in D major the notes D, E and F♯ are diatonic.

Diminished 7th chord. A four-note chord made up of superimposed minor 3rds.

Diminished interval. An interval that is one semitone narrower than a minor or perfect interval. A diminished 4th (e.g. G♯–C) is one semitone narrower than a perfect 4th (G–C); a diminished 6th (e.g. B–G♭) is one semitone narrower than a minor 6th (B–G).

Diminution. The shortening of the rhythmic values of a previously-heard melody (e.g. where ♩ ♪♪ has become ♩ ♫).

Disjunct. Melodic movement by leap rather than by step. Opposite of **conjunct**.

Dissonance. Strictly speaking, any note not belonging to a triad in root position or first inversion (even the 4th above the bass in a second inversion counts as dissonant). Some dissonances, particularly suspensions and appoggiaturas, add tension, which in early music had to be 'resolved'; others, notably passing and auxiliary notes, provide rhythmic and melodic decoration.

Dominant 7th chord. A four-note chord built on the dominant (fifth) note of the scale. It includes the dominant triad plus a minor 7th above the root.

Dorian mode. A scale that uses the following pattern of tones (T) and semitones (s): T–s–T–T–T–s–T. When starting on D, it consists of all the white notes within one octave on a keyboard.

Double-stopping. The playing of two notes simultaneously on adjacent strings of a string instrument. The term is sometimes used loosely to cover three- and four-note multiple stopping. *See also* **Triple-stopping**.

Drone. A sustained note (or notes frequently forming an interval of a 5th) held in one part while other parts play or sing melodies against it.

Dynamics. How loudly or softly the music is played; the volume of the music. Indicated by dynamic markings such as *piano* (quiet) and *crescendo* (gradually get louder).

Enlightenment. This term refers to a movement in the 18th century characterised by the exercise of reason and a critical reaction to established forms of religion. Leading enlightenment figures in France included Voltaire and Diderot, and in the United Kingdom, the Scottish philosopher David Hume.

Exposition. The first section of a **sonata form** movement, typically including the first subject in the tonic and the second subject in a related key.

Fall off. In jazz, a short downward slide ending in silence.

False relation. The occurrence of the ordinary and chromatically altered versions of the same note (such as F♮ and F♯) in two different parts at the same time, or in close proximity.

Figured bass. A figured bass is an instrumental bass part with 'figures' or 'figuring' (chiefly numerals and sharp, flat and natural signs) designed to show a continuo keyboard or lute player what type of chord to play.

First inversion. *See* **Inversion**.

Fragmentation. The splitting up of melodic lines into shorter components, which are then treated in isolation.

Fugal. *See* **Fugue**.

Fugato. A passage in **fugal** style which forms part of a larger piece of music.

Fugue. A type of piece in which a main theme called a 'subject' is treated in imitation by all the parts. 'Episodes' are the contrasting sections which depart from this pattern.

Functional harmony. A type of harmony that gravitates to the tonic through use of a hierarchy of chords, the dominant being second only to the tonic, and cadences.

Gamelan. An ensemble from Indonesia (usually Bali or Java) consisting largely of tuned percussion.

Glissando. A slide from one pitch to another.

Ground bass. Also called a ground. A bass **ostinato** or constantly repeating bass pattern, above which a melody unfolds. A popular genre of the early- and mid-Baroque period.

Half-valving. The partial opening of a valve on a brass instrument to result in a weak tone and unfocused pitch. The technique is particularly used in jazz.

Harmonics. A technique of lightly touching the string (e.g. on a violin) to produce a high, flute-like sound.

Hemiola. The articulation of two units of triple time (strong–weak–weak, strong–weak–weak) as three units of duple time (strong–weak, strong–weak, strong–weak).

Heterophony. A type of texture in which a melody is performed simultaneously with one or more rhythmically and/or melodically varied versions of itself.

Homophony. A texture in which one part has a melody and the other parts accompany, in contrast to contrapuntal writing, where each part has independent melodic and rhythmic interest.

Homorhythm. *See* **Chordal**.

Idée fixe. A term associated originally with Berlioz's music, signifying a recurring musical **motif**.

Imitation. Where a melodic idea in one part is immediately repeated in another part (exactly or inexactly), at the same or a different pitch, while the first part continues. Described with the adjective imitative.

Imperfect cadence. An open-ended cadence in which the dominant chord (V) is preceded by any other suitable chord, often I, ii or IV.

Impressionism. A compositional movement that began in France in the late 19th century and continued into the 20th, and was in some respects similar to the art movement of the same name. Important characteristics of Impressionist music include heightened attention to timbre, colour and atmosphere, non-functional harmony and tonality and fluid metre.

Improvisation. Characteristic of jazz, the spontaneous creation of new music, often based on existing musical material (such as a chord pattern).

Incidental music. Music usually written for stage, film or television, which establishes an appropriate atmosphere for the action it accompanies.

Interrupted cadence. A cadence most frequently consisting of chords V–VI, designed to defeat expectations by avoiding chord I.

Inversion (harmonic). When a chord has a note other than the root in the lowest part, it is an inversion. In a first-inversion chord the 3rd of the chord is in the lowest part, and in a second-inversion chord the 5th. For example, a triad of F major in first inversion is A–C–F, and in second inversion is C–F–A. *See also* **Root position**.

Inversion (melodic). When a melody line is heard upside down, e.g. pitches C–E–D are presented as C–A–B.

Inverted pedal. A pedal note which is held in a higher part of the texture, rather than in the bass.

Ionian mode. A scale that uses the following pattern of tones (T) and semitones (s): T–T–s–T–T–T–s. When starting on C, it consists of all the white notes within one octave on a keyboard.

Leading note. The seventh degree of a major or minor scale, usually with a strong tendency to rise to the tonic.

Leitmotif. A theme that is associated with a character, situation, mood, object or idea, especially in the operas of Richard Wagner and dramatic works/film music of later composers.

Libretto. The script or words for a dramatic work that is set to music (e.g. an **opera**, musical or oratorio).

Lydian mode. A scale that uses the following pattern of tones (T) and semitones (s): T–T–T–s–T–T–s. When starting on F, it consists of all the white notes within one octave on a keyboard. When the fourth is raised in a major scale, this is sometimes termed a Lydian inflection.

Melismatic. The setting of several notes to one syllable.

Melody-dominated homophony. A melody and accompaniment texture in which the accompaniment is not strictly chordal.

Metre. The metre refers to the pulse of the music and is indicated by the time signature.

Miniature. A short instrumental piece that depicts a scene or represents a mood.

Minimalism. A 20th- and 21st-century often deliberately simple style of composing based on repetitions of short melodic and rhythmic patterns. It was developed by American composers such as Steve Reich, Philip Glass and Terry Riley.

Mixolydian. One of the modes; this mode is the same as a major scale, except for its lowered seventh note, i.e. the scale running from G to G on the white notes of the piano.

Modal. A term often used to refer to music based on a mode rather than on major and minor keys.

Modulation. A change of key, or the process of changing key.

Monody. A term used in connection with early Baroque music in particular, referring to a solo vocal line accompanied by continuo instruments only.

Monophony. Music consisting only of a single melodic line. Also described with the adjective 'monophonic'.

Motet. A type of church music for choir, sometimes accompanied by organ, and occasionally by larger forces. A motet often has Latin words (commonly from the Bible), and is particularly but not exclusively associated with Roman Catholic services. Motets were often composed for specific occasions, unlike the Ordinary of the Mass.

Motif. A short but distinctive musical idea that is developed in various ways in order to create a longer passage of music. The adjective is 'motivic'.

Moto perpetuo. A piece or part of a piece built on constant rapid movement.

Neapolitan 6th chord. A chromatic chord (often in a minor key) consisting of the first inversion of the major chord formed on the flattened supertonic, i.e. the second degree of the scale (in D minor, for example, the Neapolitan 6th has the notes G–B♭–E♭).

Obbligato. A prominent (and essential – 'obligatory') instrumental part in Baroque music, often in an aria, in addition to the vocal part and **continuo**.

Opera. A large-scale dramatic work for singers and instrumentalists in which the whole text is sung.

Ornamentation. Addition of melodic decoration, often through the use of conventional forms such as trills and mordents.

Ostinato. A repeating melodic, harmonic or rhythmic motif, heard continuously throughout part or the whole of a piece.

Parallelism. Also known as parallel harmony, this is the parallel movement of two or more melodic lines or chords.

Passing note. A non-harmony note approached and quitted by step in the same direction, often filling in a melodic gap of a 3rd (e.g. A between G and B, where both G and B are harmony notes).

Pedal (note). A sustained or repeated note, usually in a low register, over which changing harmonies occur. A pedal on the fifth note of the scale (a dominant pedal) tends to create a sense of expectation in advance of a perfect cadence; a pedal on the keynote (a tonic pedal) can create a feeling of repose.

Pentatonic. A scale made up of five notes, most frequently the first, second, third, fifth and sixth degrees of a major scale (for example, C pentatonic is C–D–E–G–A).

Perfect cadence. A cadence consisting of the dominant chord (V or V^7) followed by the tonic (I).

Periodic phrasing. In Classical-period music particularly, where phrases of regular length are heard in balanced structures. The expression 'antecedent and consequent' is sometimes applied to these phrases.

Phrygian cadence. A type of imperfect cadence, in which the dominant chord (V) is preceded by the first inversion of the subdominant (IVb). It is used chiefly in minor keys, and particularly in Baroque music.

Pitch bend. In jazz, a microtonal variation in pitch.

Pizzicato (often abbreviated to **pizz.**). A direction to pluck, instead of bow, string(s) on a violin, viola, cello or double bass. Cancelled by the direction 'arco' - with the bow.

Plagal cadence. A cadence consisting of the subdominant chord followed by the tonic (IV–I).

Pointillism. Originally referring to a painting technique, in which small dots of colour are carefully placed to create a larger image, this refers to a musical effect in which different notes are played or sung in isolation from each other, rather than as part of a musical line, thereby sketching out a larger musical form.

Polyphony. Sometimes used as an alternative term for **counterpoint**, especially in relation to Renaissance music.

Polyrhythm. The use of more than one rhythm at the same time, often implying the presence of different metres.

Post-modernism. A style of composition that deliberately contrasts itself with modernist concepts, and the highly intellectual approach (typified by serialism) associated with them. Post-modernism tries to avoid categorising music rigidly, and often incorporates fragments of works and references to other cultures in a more approachable style.

Programmatic. Music with a stimulus that comes from outside the music itself.

Quartal harmony. Harmony based on the interval of a 4th (e.g. with chords such as A–D–G), rather than on the interval of a 3rd as in triads and 7th chords.

Quarter tone. Half a semitone.

Recapitulation. In **sonata form**, the section which follows the **development**. It is often closely based on the **exposition**, but normally both opens and closes in the tonic key.

Recitative. A piece for solo voice in an **opera**, **cantata** or oratorio (often before an aria) in which clear projection of words is the main concern. In many recitatives the music is functional rather than of great interest in itself, with the accompaniment often just for **continuo**.

Retrograde. The pitches of a previously heard melody or rhythm presented in reverse order.

Riff. In popular music styles, a short repeating phrase.

Ritornello form. A structure used in Baroque music in which an opening instrumental section (called the ritornello) introduces the main musical ideas. This returns, often in shortened versions and in related keys, between passages for one or more soloists. The complete ritornello (or a substantial part of it) returns in the tonic key at the end.

Rondo. A form in which the main theme (or subject) returns periodically in the tonic key. Simple rondo takes the form A–B–A–C–A etc., while Sonata rondo involves recapitulation of a second subject as well as the first: A–B(related key)–A–C(development)–A–B(tonic)–A. This form came to be used frequently in finales.

Root position. A chord that has the root in the lowest sounding part.

Rounded binary form. A variation of simple **binary form** (AB), in which a thematic reference to the beginning of the moment is made at the end of the B section.

Rubato. The variation of pulse by subtle lengthening and shortening of notes, so producing a free rhythmic feel.

Saltarello. A lively dance in $\frac{6}{8}$ which originated from Naples in the 13th century.

Scherzo. A fast movement which eventually replaced the minuet of the Classical era.

Secondary dominant. A passing or temporary dominant hinting at a different key, e.g. in C major, an E major chord acting as dominant to a tonic of A minor.

Secondary 7th. A 7th chord built on a degree of the scale other than the dominant.

Second inversion. *See* **Inversion**.

Sequence. Immediate repetition of a melodic or harmonic idea at a different pitch.

Siciliano. A type of movement found particularly in 17th- and 18th-century music characterised by a slow $\frac{6}{8}$ or $\frac{12}{8}$ time signature. It often included dotted rhythms.

Simple time. A metre in which the main beat is sub-divided into two equal portions. Opposite of **compound time**.

Singspiel. A type of German language opera with spoken dialogue in place of the recitative that separates the arias, ensemble numbers and choruses in other types of opera

Sonata. An instrumental work, commonly in three or four movements. From the late Baroque period onwards, sonatas are usually for solo keyboard or for single melody instrument and keyboard. 'Trio sonatas' (middle to late Baroque) are normally for two violins and continuo.

Sonata form. Typical first movement form of the Classical and Romantic periods. In three sections – **exposition**, **development**, **recapitulation** – often based on two groups of melodic material in two contrasting keys (first subject, second subject).

Stretto. The overlapping of imitative entries more closely than had previously occurred, used especially in connection with **fugal** writing.

Strophic form. A structure found mainly in simple songs in which the same music is used for each of several verses. The form can be expressed as AAA... etc.

Substitution chord. A chord that is substituted for another chord for the sake of variety. In particular the term is used in jazz.

Suspension. A suspension occurs at a change of chord, when one part hangs on to (or repeats) a note from the old chord, creating a clash, after which the delayed part resolves by step (usually down) to a note of the new chord.

Swung rhythm. In jazz and other popular music, a certain freedom in performance whereby rhythms that might in other contexts be played 'straight' as equal notes are performed with the first of each pair longer than the second, often giving a kind of triplet effect.

Syllabic. The setting of one note to one syllable.

Symphony. A work for orchestra with several (usually three or four) movements in different tempi – in effect a sonata for orchestra rather than for one or a few instruments.

Syncopation. The shifting of stress from a strong to a weak beat.

Ternary form. A musical structure of three sections in which the outer sections are similar and the central one contrasting (ABA).

Terraced dynamics. Bold, abrupt contrasts between loud and soft, with no crescendo or diminuendo marks. Mid-volume dynamics, such as *mp* and *mf*, are avoided

Tertiary progression. When roots of chords or key areas proceed by 3rds.

Tessitura. A specific part of a singer's or instrument's range. For example a 'high tessitura' indicates a high part of the range.

Texture. The relationship between the various simultaneous lines in a passage of music, dependent on such features as the number and function of the parts and the spacing between them.

Through-composed. Applied to music in which the composer avoids repetition of previous material, i.e. fresh material for different phrases in a vocal work.

Tierce de Picardie. A major 3rd in the final tonic chord of a passage in a minor key.

Timbre. The element of music concerned with the actual sound quality, or tone colour, of the music.

Tonality. Music is described as being tonal when one note is of central importance, other notes being subordinate. The note of central importance is termed the tonic when major and minor keys and scales are used. In 18th-and 19th-century music tonality is established and maintained by functional harmony, but tonality can be based instead on other types of scales, notably modes.

Transition. A linking passage.

Tremolo. A rapid and continuous repetition of a single note or two alternating notes.

Trill. An ornament in which two adjacent notes rapidly and repeatedly alternate (the note bearing the trill sign and the one above it). The symbol for trill is **tr**.

Tripartite form. A three-part form, typically A-B-C (as in 16th and 17th century pavane and galliard dance movements), as distinct from ternary form (A-B-A) movements.

Triple-stopping. The playing of three notes simultaneously (or as near simultaneously as possible) on adjacent strings of a string instrument. *See also* **Double-stopping**.

Triplet. A group of three equal notes played in the time normally taken by two notes of the same type.

Tritone. An interval that is equivalent to three tones (an augmented 4th or dimished 5th).

Turn. A four-note ornament that 'turns' around the main note. It starts on the note above, drops to the main note, drops to the note below and then returns to the main note. Indicated by the symbol ∾.

Twelve-bar blues. A standard chord sequence used in the blues and other popular music, which is based on the tonic (I), subdominant (IV) and dominant (V) chords of a key. Its most common form is I–I–I–I, IV–IV–I–I, V–IV–I–I.

Unison. Simultaneous performance of the same note or melody by two or more players or singers.

Walking bass. A bass part that persistently uses the same note length.

Whole-tone scale. A scale in which the interval between every successive note is a whole tone.

Acknowledgements:

The Duchess
Music by Rachel Portman, © Copyright 2008
Berkeley Music Publishing Co.,
Bucks Music Group Ltd. All Rights Reserved.
International Copyright Secured.

Batman Returns
Music by Daniel Elfman, © Copyright 1992
Warner-Barham Music LLC, Universal/
MCA Music Limited. All Rights Reserved.
International Copyright Secured.